Evidential Details

The

Evidential Details Mystery Series

Star Gate Battle Book

Seeds/McMoneagle

The Logistics News Network, llc.

Copywrite 2020

Evidential Details

Civil War Lost Order

"Received your book yesterday and thought I'd look at it briefly as I had things to do. But once I opened it, I kept reading it. Amazing ...fascinating"

"I'm not really all that clued on the civil war, however it was a great example of operational RV [Remote Viewing] by Joe [McMoneagle] ...and very well researched by yourself. I enjoyed it immensely.

"I found the book to be very intriguing and enjoyed it. Thank you. The existence of such people [like McMoneagle] is quite extraordinary."

Custer and Crazy Horse

I liked the Crazy Horse portrait - a first. New information - Terry and Custer - interesting revelations.

...the information about the strange way Terry's diary was transcribed struck me as obvious attempt at censoring the real data. There is an "agenda" at work here, and it is very plain.

I liked reading about what happened. I had never read much about that battle, just thought it was Custer's group fighting many Indians, etc. You do a good job of bringing the reader into the situation. Your photos were wonderful.

[The] Custer picture is fine; one can easily imagine the real man. Crazy Horse portrait is striking, and when combined with the biographical information you provide, I can believe this is the guy. A wonderful portrait.

I've read most of this series. In this case, I got more of a sense of Custer and the battle, not just from what Joe viewed, but also from Seeds' surrounding text.

Evidential Details

The Quick Take

(The) authority to award the Legion of Merit Medal is reserved for general officers and flag officers in pay grade O-9 (e.g., [for] Lieutenant General and Vice Admiral) and above... https://en.wikipedia.org/wiki/Legion_of_Merit

The U.S. Army's Legion of Merit Medal Bestowal Requirements

At least two witnesses must submit seven military forms for determination as to the proper medal. Based on the quality of the information, Military Decorations personnel selected the medal with the following language.

The award is given for service rendered in a clearly exceptional manner. For service not related to actual war the term "key individual" applies to a narrower range of positions than in time of war and requires evidence of significant achievement. In peacetime, service should be in the nature of a special requirement or of an extremely difficult duty performed in an unprecedented and clearly exceptional manner.

Once it was documented what this soldier could do, these Services requested his services:

During his career, Mr. McMoneagle has provided ...informational support to the Central Intelligence Agency (CIA), Defense Intelligence Agency (DIA), National Security Agency (NSA), Drug Enforcement Agency (DEA), Secret Service, Federal Bureau of Investigation (FBI), United States Customs (ICE),the National Security Council (NSC), most major commands (Army, Navy, Air Force, Intelligence) within the Department of Defense (DOD), and hundreds of other individuals, companies, and corporations.

Paragraph from Mr. McMoneagle's CV.

Evidential Details

Medals Received

Legion of Merit

Meritorious Service

Citations

Meritorious Service with **one** Oak Leaf Cluster;[1]
Army Commendation with **two** Oak Leaf Clusters, Presidential Unit;
Meritorious Unit with **three** Oak Leaf Clusters;
Vietnam Gallantry Cross with Palm for gathering enemy intelligence for Allied counter offensives.

Evidential Details

The Bronze Plaque on the Veterans Memorial Wall

In what is clearly the most fascinating component of U.S. Military History, Joseph McMoneagle is the only man in history to be awarded medals for consistent accuracy in Remote Viewing (Psy-functioning) by a military. As *Operation Star Gate's* Number 1 Military Intelligence asset at Fort Meade, Maryland, he was the Pentagon's go to man when secret data could not be obtained by any other means or was time sensitive.

The Evidential Details Mysteries Series

Copyright 2020 by LNN, llc.
All rights reserved

**Published on the Evidential Details Imprint,
a Division of Logistics News Network, LLC.**
inbox@LNN1.com

Star Gate Battle Book ISBN: ISBN 978-0-9826928-8-2

Civil War Lost Order ISBN: 978-0-9826928-6–8

United States – History – Civil War, 1861-865 - Generals, United States – Civil War Campaigns – Civil War Correspondence – Battles, South Mountain, Harper's Ferry - 19th Century Military Intelligence - U.S. Military Intelligence - Remote Viewing – Joseph McMoneagle – Anomalous Cognition – Stanford Research Institute – Dr. Harold Puthoff - Library of Congress Card Number: 2011905178

Custer and Crazy Horse ISBN: 978-0-9826928-4–4

United States – History – Indian Wars – 1876 – Dakota Indians – Little Big Horn Battle Field, Battles of the 1876 Yellowstone campaign - Custer, George Armstrong, 1839 –1876 – Generals, United States – United States Calvary – August Belmont

Book design by LNN. Printed in the United States of America

If you are unable to purchase our books in a bookstore,
they are available at our web site at: www.EvidentialDetails.com

All rights reserved. No part of this book may be reproduced or transmitted in any form or by means, electronic or mechanical, including photo-copying or by any information storage and retrieval system without the written permission of the Publisher under International and Pan American Copyright Conventions.

Any interpretations or historical conclusions contained herein cannot be considered to represent the opinion of, or to be endorsed by Joseph McMoneagle or any other individual. The final manuscript was not submitted for approval. There was no prior knowledge of when the manuscript was to be made available or the manner in which this research would be brought forward.

In the event of inaccurate picture credit, kindly contact us with the corrected information and/or verifiable proof of ownership, for an immediate correction. Word *only* portions, of this book may be reproduced for academic dissertations or in non-fiction works within the legally established Fair Use guidelines and proper crediting. Due to the nature of the material, no text may be altered.

Pictures on the Internet and the Millennium Copywrite Act of 2000, on the heels of the Sony Bono Copyright Act, continue to be problematic. It remains an effort where organizations can only strive to be in compliance. In the event of inaccurate credit, please contact us with corrected information and proof of property ownership.

Table of Contents

The Quick Take..5

The Steel Plaque on the Brick Wall...................................7

Introduction to Remote Viewing - Diana Spencer's Auto Accident.............11

Book One

The Civil War's Greatest Mystery – the Lost Dispatch..............37

Book Two

Custer and Crazy Horse..89

Part Three

Credentials...151

The Military's "Human Use" Clearances...........................153

Encounters with the Chinese RV Program........................154

Remote Viewing Program Protocols.................................156

Operation Star Gate Beginnings.......................................160

Targeted Bookshelf..174

Additional Taskings..176

References...178

Evidential Details

The worst term of all is "psychic." No stable definition has ever been established for it, and there are great hazards in attempting to utilize a term which has not much in the way of an agreed upon definition.

Supporters do assume that it refers to extraordinary, non-normal (paranormal) activities of mind. But skeptics assume it refers to illusion, derangement and a variety of non-normal or abnormal clinical psychopathologies.

R E M O T E - V I E W I N G - One of the Superpowers of The Human Bio-Mind;
Remote Viewing and its Conceptual Nomenclature Problems by Ingo Swann (09Jan96)

In actual practice, the psychic produces these disconnected phrases and hopes that one of them will trigger something in the customer's unconscious mind, providing the "psychic" answer. Random utterances not having a definite meaning can always be twisted and reshaped to mean virtually anything that fits the situation. There are many "psychics" who have taken this type of gibberish to a finely honed skill.

Operation Star Gate's Leonard Buchanan – *The Seventh Sense*

Det (Detachment) G's viewers looked at projects ranging from the status of a cement plant in a hostile country to the location of Soviet troops in Cuba. Important North Korean personalities were targeted, as well as underground facilities in Europe, chemical weapons in Afghanistan, the presence of electronic bugs in the new U.S. embassy in Moscow, the activities of a KGB general officer, a missing U.S. helicopter, tunnels under the Korean Demilitarized Zone, and numerous buildings whose purposes were unknown to U.S. Intelligence.

Smith, Paul H., *Reading the Enemy's Mind –
Inside Star Gate, America's Psychic Espionage Program*

Evidential Details

An

Introduction

To Remote Viewing

A review of the terminology,
history and capabilities targeting

The Former Princess Of Wales Diana Spencer's 1997 Auto Accident

(For the cover story, please refer to the Table of Contents)

"When they (University researchers) did produce an incredibly accurate response during an experiment, it was in even a moderate sense "unnerving." In a greater sense, it was "earth shattering." As (Stanford PhD) Russell (Targ) implied, for some it was even "terrifying". In no case, was it ever taken lightly, as it always had a tendency to alter one's perspective towards reality and/or our place within it."

~ Medal Recipient Joseph W. McMoneagle~

Evidential Details

It was the peak of the Twentieth Century's Cold War [1945-1990]. The United States, the old Soviet Union, and the People's Republic of China were striving to find new ways to get an intelligence edge. During the years 1968 to 1972, the United States obtained reports that scientists in the Soviet Union had had some success with a telekinesis program that introduced atrial fibulation into frog hearts causing a heart attack. Realizing the program could target key military and political leaders, and so driven by a threat assessment, the Central Intelligence Agency funded a Stanford University think tank in Menlo Park, California - the Stanford Research Institute (SRI) - to conduct an analysis about what humanity through the ages has pondered. The doctors were to determine scientifically if psy-functioning could be taught, quantified and directed within written protocols. If so, did this represent a credible threat to the people of the United States? Their highly classified "Black Ops" program lasted from early 1972 until November 1995.

Under the most extensive and stringent experimentation that two PhD's could devise, the SRI, supported by other labs and the Army, developed mankind's first "psychic" protocols. "This led to greater understanding of everything from methods of evaluation, to establishing statistical standards, to how a human brain might be appropriately studied."[i] When their findings were made public, many in the academic community were privately stunned.

Eventually this covert military effort focused on real world data collection. As the years of research, analysis and application moved through the 1970's and 80's, Army brass with wholly personal motives, would attempt to quash the program even when research costs did not impact their budget. "All the funding had been approved on a year-to-year basis, and only then based on how effective the unit was in supporting the tasking agencies. These reviews were made semi-annually at the Senate and House select subcommittee level, where the work results were reviewed within the context in which it was happening."[ii]

Fortunately, for The People, the program was given different code names and moved around various Defense budgets until much of the research and development was completed. What emerged was an incredibly "robust" database - and a process - referred to as Controlled Remote Viewing [CRV].[1] [This may also stand for Coordinate Remote Viewing when longitudinal and latitudinal target coordinates are used.]]

Much of the work took place within the 902nd United States Army Intelligence Group at Fort Meade, Maryland, whose barracks have been demolished. However, from the fastidiously maintained database emerged statistically advanced practitioners; world class viewers whose RV data was the "best in the business." Among these, one remote viewer was the first in history to be decorated with the Army's Legion of Merit and Meritorious Service Awards (with five Oak Leaf Clusters) for having made key contributions to the Intelligence community. This same individual was tasked to unlock the mysteries in this Evidential Details Book Series.

Obviously, accuracy is the name of the game. As with any horizon application process, purposefully moving the human brain into what may be a matrix system at the sub-quark level required new clinical terminology. As the CRV process was tested, protocols written and cautiously modified, scientists documented mental hazards to viewer accuracy. These hindrances were cataloged and their characteristics differentiated. Year after year laboratory research determined accurate mental representations could be inhibited in a variety of ways. Some of these mental distracters included:

Physical Inclemency - Knowledge of an expected disruption like a phone call or someone about to arrive during a remote viewing session.

Advanced Visuals - A thought you cannot get rid of before a session.

Emotional Distracters or Attractors - An image you do or do not want to view regardless of the tasking.

Front Loading - Knowledge of what the target is before the viewing session. If localized, it can be used in targeting a feature within the whole picture, perhaps a house in a meadow in front of a mountain. However, without neutral wording like "The target is man-made" the object is generally rendered unworkable.

Analytic Overlay [AOL] - If a viewer is not informed about the target and not front loaded but still has personal information about it, that knowledge may pollute the information stream rendering the session unworkable. Analytic Overlay can be a problem for any viewer. According to the military's former #1 remote viewer:

Joseph McMoneagle - Analytic overlay - CRV [Controlled Remote Viewing], **as a format or method for learning remote viewing, offers a structure within which you can discard or identify specific elements within a session for which you are certain or not certain. Analytic Over-Lay (AOL) being a common label for something that falls within the "uncertain" category. However, when studied (under laboratory conditions), there is evidence that fifty percent of the time, information labeled as AOL actuality, wasn't.**

I have observed just as many times, someone being smacked up against the side of the head while attempting CRV because they had strayed from the given format and slipped into AOL. I think that sometimes you may forget that CRV was developed within the hallowed halls of SRI and was taught there for years. I saw very little

Evidential Details

difference in the AOL pitfalls with CRV and other methodologies. I did see that to some extent it was a highly polished technique, which was more easily transferred through training.

With this quick review of the subconscious transference of recollections, we turn to the remote viewing of the Princess Diana Spencer's accident in the early morning hours of August 31, 1997. As this researcher found, how one targets is critical to the result. In the fall of 1997, the massive press coverage of Princess Diana's accident and funeral emerged as a very real overlay problem. The Hotel Ritz in Paris, France rather than the crash site was targeted. There had been much less news coverage at the hotel. At the time, this target was less than two months old. No accident report had been completed. An envelope, with a second target envelope inside, had been mailed to Joseph McMoneagle's home with nothing more than the targeting coordinates and a date. A skeptical *Life Magazine* reporter was on hand as an observer to write a story.

Mr. McMoneagle had requested I submit a target. The viewing event started at 11:49 am on October 29, 1997. What makes these sessions interesting is that the reader can sense the Intelligence intellect. Having viewed 1200 targets in just the last two years of the military's Operation Star Gate alone, this job would reasonably have been assigned to the only viewer to participate in the program for twenty-three years. What was submitted was:

Target Envelope No. 102997 - (no additional information other than what's sealed within the envelope.)

* * *

As her size nine shoes hit the airport tarmac the former Princess of Wales Diana Spencer, 36, knew she was entitled to an escort by that special branch of the French Interior Ministry charged with guarding visiting dignitaries - the Service de Protection des Hautes Personalities (SPHP). But there would be no need of the service once she left the airport. This was to be a private visit.

Diana was returning from a yachting vacation in the Mediterranean off Northeast Sardinia. She and Emad "Dodi" Al-Fayed, [1955-1997] had been aboard the Fayed family's $27 million dollar (US$39.5m/2015), 195 foot yacht *Jonikal,* with 16 crew members.

At this point, "…in her relationship with Dodi Fayed she was displaying a new facet. In some ways a late developer, she had grown up and was simply having some adult fun."[iii] But the couple had been stalked by high-speed paparazzi boats wherever they went. On their last afternoon, they came ashore at the Cala de Volpe in Sardinia and the, "Paparazzi

Evidential Details

swarmed around them like bees, flashing away."[iv] Forced back to the boat, "Things came to a head when a scuffle broke out between three paparazzi and several members of the *Jonikal*'s crew."[v]

At about the same time, hundreds of miles away, a 73 year-old grandfather, Edward Williams, walked into the police station in Mountain Ash, Mid Glamorgan, Wales. He reported to the police he had had a premonition Princess Diana was going to die. The police log, time stamped 14:12 hours on August 27, 1997, stated:

"He [Williams] *said he was a psychic and predicted that Princess Diana was going to die. In previous years he has predicted that the Pope and Ronald Reagan were going to be the victims of assassination. On both occasions he was proven to be correct. Mr. Williams appeared to be quite normal."*[vi]

Based on his previous record the police passed this report along to the department's Special Branch Investigative Unit.

Fed up with the non-stop press hassle, on Saturday August 30, Dodi and Diana boarded the Fayed's Gulfstream IV jet at Olbia airport in Sardinia and flew north. They arrived at Le Bourget Airport about 10 miles north of Paris, France at 3:20 p.m. Fayed's butler Rene Delorm recalled, "Unfortunately, we had a welcoming committee of about ten paparazzi waiting for us."[vii] About 600 feet (183 meters) away was a Mercedes and a Range Rover. "We had all seen the paparazzi, so we moved quickly. We wanted to get out of the plane and into the cars as fast as possible. (Body Guard) Trevor (Rees-Jones) was the first out of the jet..."[viii]

The entourage had a police escort from the airport up to France's highway A-1 leading to Paris. But as they entered the expressway, reporter's cars and two man motorcycle teams immediately dogged the entourage. The paparazzi were armed with powerful, maximum strength, flashes to penetrate deep into the car. Philippe Dourneau, 35, was Dodi's chauffeur. But in the Range Rover vehicle there had been a switch. At the wheel was the Assistant Chief of Hotel Security Henri Paul. It is unclear why Paul was chauffeuring and not at the Ritz Hotel as acting Security Chief.

Once on the highway, Dodi instructed Ritz Hotel driver Dourneau to pick up speed in an attempt to elude photographers. What ensued was a high-speed pursuit with motorcycle cameramen weaving in and out shooting pictures. The motorcycle whirl was so intense Diana reportedly cried out in alarm that someone could get killed.[ix]

The photographer's strategy was to slow the convoy down. "Then a black car sped ahead of us and ducked in front of the Mercedes, braking and making us slow down so the paparazzi on motorcycles could get more pictures. They were risking their lives and ours, just to get a shot of Dodi and

Evidential Details

Diana riding in a car. "*Unbelievable*", exclaimed butler Rene Delorm.[x]

Dodi was not accustomed to this and after their high seas harassment, his patience was running thin. Pursuing for miles, the paparazzi then used phones to notify photographers ahead to form another gauntlet on the next highway segment. The Fayed cars split up in an attempt to divide the photographers. Some pursued Henri Paul as he drove to Dodi's apartment to deliver the luggage.

Finally, the Mercedes made it to Bois de Boulogne on the outskirts of Paris to visit the Fayed's Windsor Villa. They arrived about 3:45 p.m. Then they were off to the Ritz Hotel in downtown Paris at 4:35. Alerted by the cameramen the hotel entrance was by now packed with photographers which in turn generated curiosity seekers in the general public.

Once inside the hotel, Diana checked into the second floor Imperial Suite and went to have her hair done. She also made some phone calls. After the accident, London's *Daily Mail* correspondent Richard Kay stated that Diana had called him saying she was going to complete her contractual obligations through November and then go into private life.

Another call was made to psychic Rita Rogers whom Diana had been in contact with since 1994. Three weeks earlier, on August 12, Dodi and Di had visited Rogers for a reading on Dodi. She warned him not to go driving in Paris. "*I saw a tunnel, motorcycles, there was this tremendous sense of speed.*"[xi] Uneasy, Rogers reminded Diana about her readout concerning a Parisian tunnel saying, "*...remember what I told Dodi.*"[xii]

At seven o'clock, they left the hotel for Dodi's apartment at Rue 1 Arsene-Houssaye arriving at 7:15 p.m. Here the couple found the street so crowded they could not even open the car door. "The paparazzi literally mobbed the couple," said (32 year old former Royal Marine Kes) Wingfield. "They really disturbed and frightened the Princess, even though she was used to this. These paparazzi were shouting, which made them even more frightening. I had to push them back physically.'"[xiii]

From their third floor apartment, butler Rene recalled:

"*...I could see they were being mobbed. I heard the shouting, saw the flashes going off and watched a security guard shove one of the photographers. Dodi did his best to shield Diana as Trevor and Kes fought to clear a path to the door... The princess was ashen and trembling, and Dodi was angry as they stalked through the apartment door...*"[xiv]

This was the way it was going to be. Rumors were rife about a marriage proposal and some wealthy publishers made it clear big money was available to the photographer that got the "million dollar shot". But no million dollars was ever budgeted.

Later, after things settled down and Dodi had returned from shopping

Evidential Details

for two rings at the Repossi Jewelry Boutique, Rene recounted, "I met Dodi as he walked through the kitchen doorway, his eyes gleaming with excitement. It was then that he showed me the ring. *'Make sure we have champagne on ice when we come back from dinner,'* he told me urgently. *'I'm going to propose to her tonight!'*"[xv] Elated, he also phoned this proposal news to his cousin Hassan Yassin that evening.[xvi] [Dodi received a US$100,000/month ($146.5/2015) allowance from his father.]

Dodi had the Hotel staff book a 9:45 p.m. dinner reservation at the fashionable restaurant Chez Benoit on the Rue Saint Martin. He also phoned the Ritz staff he would not be returning. As a result, Security Chief Henri Paul departed for the weekend at 7:05 p.m.

At 9:30 p.m., Dodi and Diana left for dinner but could not get through the crowd at the restaurant entrance. It was clear they could not enter a restaurant together. The enormous number of paparazzi forced Dodi to cancel their night out. The Press was controlling his special night with his special lady. A frustrated Dodi decided they should make the four mile drive to the Hotel Ritz where they could dine in France's only "safe" restaurant. But Security Chief Henri Paul had gone for the weekend and the abrupt change in plans left the hotel staff with no time to prepare for their arrival.

When they arrived at the Ritz, another press riot broke out. It took Diana two whole minutes to negotiate the camera gauntlet the 20 feet from the front door drive-up to the hotel turnstile. The security camera time stamped her entrance at 9:53 p.m. Security man Wingfield said: *"I had to protect her physically from the paparazzi, who were coming really too close to her. Their cameras were right next to her face."*[xvii]

Dodi was now furious and started shouting at his employees about no security to shield the 10-second walk up from the driveway. Shaken, the press savvy Diana wept in the lobby. Everyone was upset. With the owner's son angry, and the security force completely embattled, a decision was made to call the Security Chief back to work. Francois Tendil called Henri Paul's cell phone at 9:55 p.m.

Once in their hotel room, Dodi called his father Mohammed Al-Fayed at approximately 10:00 p.m. He said the two would announce their engagement the next week when Diana returned from England.[xviii] "Diana always had the children for the last few days before they went back to school at the start of a new term, so that she could get everything ready and make sure they had the right kit."[xix] On Friday, she had called to confirm her boys would be at the airport to meet her on Sunday morning.

Dinner was ordered from the hotel's Imperial Suite restaurant. Diana's last meal was scrambled eggs with mushrooms and asparagus, then vegetable tempura with fillet of sole. As Di and Dodi were trying to dine

Evidential Details

normally, Henri Paul was pushing his way through the paparazzi into the hotel. And two months later, as Mr. McMoneagle looked at a double blind envelope on his dining room table, he began:

McMoneagle – I find myself standing next to a man who is inside some kind of a public building. He is approximately five feet, ten inches in height, good build, good condition physically. He weighs about 165 pounds, is clean shaven, light brown hair, right handed, 38-40 years of age, and is not British or American; meaning he probably has another language other than English as his native tongue.[1]

Upon his return, Henri Paul waited around the Ritz for about two hours. He allegedly had a couple drinks at the bar. The Ritz security cameras recorded his behavior which would be used for future analysis. As Chief of Security, he was certainly aware of their placement and recording abilities.

McMoneagle - Building interior - Where he (Paul) is within the building is inside of a very elaborate corridor. It runs the full length of the building and has lots of gilded paint, mirrors, thick carpets, lots of flowers, and is very fancy. The corridor runs straight out to a front entry which is well lit and very busy (even though my sense is that it is very late at night). There is an area off to the right of this corridor which has a lot of dark paneling and dark colors with a long bar or type of counter. So, this may be the reception area of the hotel or something like that.

Where he (Paul) is standing is where the main corridor intersects with a short corridor that runs off at a ninety degree angle to the left. It intersects with some kind of a smaller staff or receiving area; perhaps a back door to the building. It is recessed and that is where his car is parked.

The Etoile Limousine Company manager Jean-Francis Musa, 39, provided six cars to the Ritz Hotel for their exclusive use. This Mercedes was licensed as a Grande Remise auto meaning only a licensed chauffeur was authorized to drive it. Henri Paul did not possess those credentials.

McMoneagle - Driver orientation - I believe that he (Paul) drives a cab or limo...on the side, because I associate him with a car, which is parked outside and he is thinking about this car, or it seems to occupy his thoughts for some reason. He is mostly interested with driving from point A to point B. I believe he is not alone and get a strong feeling of mixed male/female in energy; which either means his passenger will be gay, or consist of two people -- a male and a female.

Limo is not a stretch limo but a short, black and formal kind of

---

[1] Paul was 167 lbs. and he was 41 years old. He had brown hair and was also balding. His native language was French. He spoke fluent English and some German.

car. **I get an impression of a Mercedes emblem or some kind of emblem like that, so I'm assuming it is a very expensive car, could be a Mercedes. It is formal and black with an extended foot space in the back seat. Four doors.** It is very heavy and my sense is that it might be equipped for important passengers — e.g., bullet proof glass, armoring, hardened tires, etc.; which leads me to believe that at least one of the passengers [Trevor Rees-Jones, 29] **might be a body-guard** [but] **this may be Analytic overlay caused by the excessive feelings of security surrounding this vehicle and driver.** [2]

* * *

Information about Henri Paul's mixed motivations have come to light in the years since the accident. Born one of five brothers on July 3, 1956 in the port town of Lorient, France, he had a Bachelors Degree in Mathematics and Science from the Lycee St. Louis and had won several contests for his skill as a classical pianist. He became a pilot in 1976 but was unable to qualify as a jet fighter pilot when he joined the French Air Force.

In 1986, Paul helped setup Ritz Security. He went on to become Assistant Director. On the day of the accident, he was carrying 12,560 francs (US $2,280) and his savings account passbook. Where the money came from is unknown, but he was one of only two men in France that had access to the automobile conversations of Dodi and Di. The ability to advise the press of their plans would have been of great value. [Henri Paul may have charged the equivalent of US$2,250 (1997) per surveillance event and simply had an additional $30 pocket money that day. His salary was reported at $40,000 ($58,600/2015) per year.]

Personal adversity. Henry Paul had recently been passed over for promotion a second time by Hotel Ritz management. The first disappointment had come on Jan 1, 1993 when the nod went to colleague Jean Hocquet even though Paul was obviously in position as the number two security man. Now again, effective June 30, 1997, as Deputy Chief, he became the defacto head of a twenty person security team while Ritz Management searched for another chief. Now vulnerable, Paul had been informed exactly one month before the accident.

---

[2] The Mercedes S 280 sedan, valued at about $100,000 (US$146.520/2015) was engineered with eight advanced safety systems. The car had a reinforced chassis and roof. It had energy absorbing front and rear end crumple zones with electronic traction control. It also had an electronic ESP sensing system, which monitored trajectory with wheel speed to sense cornering speeds.

Evidential Details

Session Sketch

This drawing provides a rare glimpse intelligence level RV artwork. In this exercise, people and not the building were targeted. But, this sketch could be the third floor at the North Korean Embassy in Moscow, Russia, or any building, anywhere, anytime. As a person was the target, the Hotel Ritz Paris first floor was roughed out at midnight on August 31, 1997. Points of interest are:

1) At the top of the page, the words **Big Bldg** appear;
2) The various circles with an **X** inside indicates where people were standing at approximately 12:15 a.m. on August 31, 1997.
3) On the left, the **Main Door** is shown with an **X** representing the doorman. As the hall extends to the right, the various rooms are notated.
4) Toward the bottom is a **Business** area. As you walk from the front door, **"There is an area off to the right of this corridor which has a lot of dark paneling and dark colors with a long bar or type of counter."**
5) At the top is an **Alcove** with two people inside. These individual's backgrounds – conversations – futures – mental states - deaths can be targeted at any time in the future.
6) Where the hallway comes to a junction there is a **Man**. This is Henri Paul as he monitors the activities in both corridors. What were Paul's private thoughts? "**I associate him with a car which is parked outside and he is thinking about this car, or it seems to occupy his thoughts for some reason.**"
7) Behind Henri Paul is the **Laborer Area**. Next to this is the drawing date and time documenting who was where when.
8) The hallway to the **Side Door**, "**...intersects with some kind of a smaller staff or receiving area; perhaps a back door to the building. It is recessed and that is where his car is parked.**" That recessed area is shown.
9) McMoneagle also shows the **Formal Black Limo**'s position by the back door and correctly identified the automobile's color and manufacturer's hood ornament. (bottom right)

Evidential Details

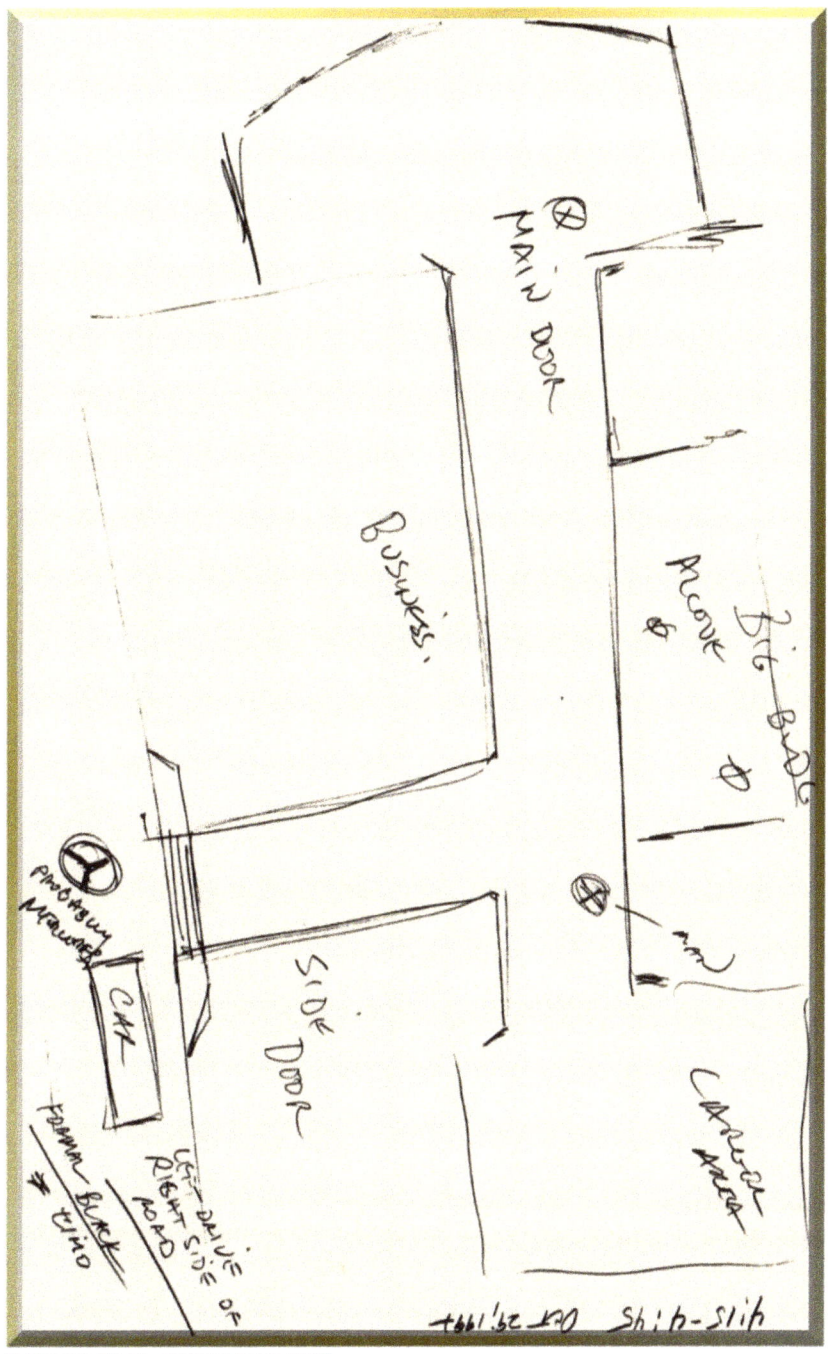

Hotel Ritz Paris first floor with Mercedes (lower right) as viewed from Virginia.

Evidential Details

Post mortem tests stated Paul had consumed two antidepressants called Fluoxetine and Tiapride before the accident. Fluoxetine is the active ingredient in Prozac and together these drugs are commonly used to fight alcoholism. When alcohol is introduced, the intoxicant effect is multiplied. On September 17, a more sophisticated laboratory's final report was issued. It stated that Henri Paul had been in, *"moderate chronic.alcoholism for a minimum of one week."*[xx] Once this became public, the Ritz's attorneys and Mohammed Al-Fayed found themselves on the defensive. An unlicensed employee now appeared criminally negligent in a multiple wrongful death accident while in Hotel Ritz employment. It became the million dollar picture vs. the Al-Fayeds

The intoxication driving limit in France is 0.50 grams per liter. One lab report stated Henri Paul's blood alcohol level was 1.87 g/l. This is the equivalent drinking time for eight or nine shots of whiskey in what was found to be an empty stomach. A second, private laboratory's more moderate findings were used in the Final Report. The Paris Prosecutor's Office Report stated:

"On this particular point, numerous expert's reports examined following the autopsy on the body of Henri Paul rapidly showed the presence of a level of pure alcohol per litre of blood of between 1.73 and 1.75 grams, which is far superior, in all cases, than the legal level.

Similarly, these analyses revealed as [did] those carried out on samples of the hair and bone marrow of the deceased, that he regularly consumed Prozac and Tiapridal, both medicines which are not recommended for drivers, as they provoke a change in the ability to be vigilant, particularly when they are taken in combination with alcohol."[xxi]

So had Henri Paul been out drinking? It is known he returned to the Ritz two hours and fifty minutes after departing. But no one knew where he was or what he was doing when he received the Ritz phone call. Subsequent investigations about who had seen Paul during this period failed to provide a single witness. In Paris, in the fall of 1997, there was a real fear of liability for anyone acknowledging Paul had been drinking in their establishment. Nonetheless, the French media reported *"someone"* saw Paul drinking "aperitifs" between 7:05 and <u>10:08</u> p.m. that evening. "Someone" is wide open. It means that after he got the call to return at <u>9:55</u> p.m., he dallied almost another quarter-hour before departing which is hard to believe given everyone's concerns. Until now, the critical question about where and what Paul was doing before returning to the hotel remains unknown.

McMoneagle - I think he was in fact sitting in a small restaurant or coffee shop, very near where he lives. Maybe even on the corner near his house. He was alone as far as I can tell. I think he was in fact

Evidential Details

drinking coffee. I do not think he was depressed, at least not more than usual. Also, regardless of what might be said, I DID NOT get a sense that he was drunk. It is remotely possible that he was taking some kind of a medication but I doubt it.

Coffee! Not drunk! This flew in the face of the formal investigation. We were now privately aware, months before the controversy started, Henri Paul was not drunk.

Henri Paul was a pilot. Research indicated it was impossible to reconcile allegations of alcoholism with Paul's recent physical examination. Unbeknownst to the authorities issuing the report, just two days before the accident, Paul had completed a "rigorous" physical examination to renew his pilot's license. His *Certificat D'Aptitude Physique et Mentale* showed, "No signs of alcoholism."[xxii] A direct medical conflict supporting McMoneagle. Was Paul really fighting alcoholism? Six months after these sessions, the Ritz Hotel security videos further reaffirmed our data.

Behavioral Psychologist Dr. Martin Skinner commented in Fulcrum Productions documentary for ITV. The doctor stated there were no behavioral signs of drunkenness as Henri Paul waited for Dodi and Diana.

Skinner: *I don't think there is evidence, from the video, that can suggest he looked drunk. The pictures of him walking up and down the corridor are straight and smooth. He is standing very still and there is nothing in his demeanor, from these videos, to suggest that there are any problems with his competence in this situation.*[xxiii]

Next came a statement from Trevor Rees-Jones, the front seat bodyguard sitting next to Paul. About intoxication, he said:

Rees-Jones: *I had no reason to suspect he was drunk. He did not look or sound like he had been drinking. He just seemed his normal self. He was working. He was competent. End of story. I can state quite categorically that he was not a hopeless drunk as some have tried to suggest. I like to think I have enough intelligence to see if the guy was plastered or not – and he wasn't.*[xxiv]

Neither the bodyguards, nor Dodi, or anyone else at the Hotel detected anything unusual in Paul's behavior. But there was more.

Paul's blood was next reported as containing abnormally high carbon monoxide levels - twenty percent too much. How this happened has never been determined. But doctors agree it is impossible for a forty year old man, with that much poison in his blood stream, not to look and feel sick - too sick for high speed urban driving. When the press advanced the idea car exhaust was the source of Paul's poisoning, Dodi's father, Mohammed

Evidential Details

Al-Fayed, put the obvious question: *"How did Henri Paul get 20% carbon monoxide in his blood when my son had none?"*[xxv]

The obvious question is how you can get that much CO_2 into someone's blood stream when, due to an instantaneous death there was no breathing, and the engine had stopped.

During his last month Henri Paul had come to know what it was like to assume the Security Chief's responsibilities while the Ritz Hotel interviewed. He must have been concerned an outside hire may not be as accommodating as his previous colleague boss had been. After setting up the Ritz security operation, and with a decade of service, Henri Paul now faced the possibility of being forced out by a new supervisor uneasy about his hotel security experience. Clearly, Ritz management was not taking care of Paul as a career professional.[3]

Another component of the Henri Paul enigma concerned the fact that most nations have an Embassy in Paris and many dignitaries and diplomats stay at the Ritz. Stories started to appear that Paul was in the employ of various "foreign and domestic" intelligence services. Then it was discovered he had one million francs [US$200,000–$250,000] spread between eighteen bank accounts in an attempt to disguise the fact. Al-Fayed would later make the claim Paul had spent at least three years working for British intelligence. Where he got this information, or if it is true, is unknown. Paul was also allegedly in contact with the Direction General de la Securite Exterieure [DGSE] - French Intelligence. So, we were left with a feigned alcoholic dead man; with employment and big money surveillance concerns; ordered to violate multiple traffic laws; by a romantically aggravated boss in love with the world's foremost beauty.

Henri Paul was uncertain about his future. He had to have been anxious about protecting his access to the Hotel Ritz time and date stamped video-monitoring system. He must have been concerned about his ability to generate good income by documenting high profile business people or foreign dignitary's arrivals and departures.

But all of a sudden, that night there was a positive side to the whole discordant affair. A rare opportunity to make a positive impression on the owner's son was at hand. In the wee hours of August 31, 1997, it would have been impossible for any driver to presume to caution a provoked Dodi Al-Fayed about safe driving on nearly deserted streets. As characterized by French Union Official Claude Luc:

---

[3] The Hotel Ritz subsequently hired a former Scotland Yard Chief Superintendent John MacNamara. His background in criminal intelligence management and investigations was substantially different than Paul's Air Force Reserve security credentials.

Evidential Details

*"If one of the Fayeds gives you an order, you follow it.
No questions asked."*[xxvi]

Whatever his prospects, Security Chief Henri Paul was illegally behind the wheel again. He was laid to rest in Lorient, France on September 20, 1997. Father Léon Théraud gave the sermon at Sainte Therese Church.

* * *

Associated Press
A back door security camera photograph time stamped 12:19 a.m. just before they departed. It shows Henri Paul (left) conversing with Dodi and Diana with Trevor Rees-Jones in the background

On Saturday night, now Sunday morning August 31, a physically aggressive horde of stalkarazzi and other onlookers, estimated at approximately 130 people, jockeyed for position at the front door of the Hotel Ritz Paris. Diana Frances Spencer and her boyfriend Dodi, son of Egyptian born multi-millionaire Mohammad Al-Fayed, needed a second vehicle to exit the hotel's back entrance. Due to the paparazzi, a front door - back door scheme had been set-up for their return to Dodi's apartment. Dodi would take Diana out the back leaving his personal Range Rover in front as a decoy.

McMoneagle – Car is parked on the right side of the road (right side driving) which would rule out England, Bahamas, Hong Kong, Japan, etc. It is night and it is dark. The time for this event is current, probably 1985 to 1997. I will try and bring that down to a shorter period later.

Evidential Details

The tag on the limo is elongated, with letters and numbers-- which is a European style of tag (License 688 LTV 75). **My sense is that there may actually be two colors of tags on this car, or that it has interchangeable tags, which are changed, dependent upon where it is being operated. One is yellow with black lettering; the other is white with black lettering. It may be that there are two different colored tags on the car simultaneously—one color on one end, one color on the other.**

This is a superb surveillance example. The yellow license with black lettering was on the rear bumper. As it turned out, the color license designated a private car. The white tag is a "for hire" vehicle.[4] From this the reader can gather the type of information available through remote viewing should this car have been driving a foreign dignitary.

After some hallway discussion, Ritz chauffeur's Philippe Dourneau and Jean-Francois Musa drove two decoy vehicles to the hotel's front door. The night was clear. The temperature was 77 degrees [25C]. Their engines were revved up as Dodi and Diana hurried out the back door at 12:20 a.m.

Diana's last few minutes on earth were now inexorably caught-up in the emotional web of her incensed boyfriend and his driver's employment needs. Some paparazzi across the Rue Cabman observed them as Trevor, Diana, and then Dodi came through the turnstile and got into the Mercedes. Henri Paul pulled out and the chase was on.

McMoneagle - Believe the car is the main focus of this target. The man [Paul] may also be of interest.... I believe this target has to do with an accident that probably occurred either in the very late night hours or possibly very early morning hours. Traffic is very light and the streets are very quiet. Get a sense that there are few cars about, in a place which is usually crawling with cars.

The Mercedes is moving very fast from what apparently is a northwest...direction. Have a sense that it goes over an overpass or cloverleaf kind of interchange which then drops straight down into a tunnel.

The car traveled toward the Seine River's westbound express street referred to as the Cours la Reine. Then they entered the Alexander III & Invalides Tunnel Bridge. The tunnel is 330 meters (361 yards) long.

McMoneagle - It [Mercedes] then exits the tunnel and covers a large curve of open road which enters another tunnel like area, only this second tunnel is not enclosed completely. Have a sense of

---

[4] In Foreign Relations, these plates could indicate a restricted territory vehicle. If unauthorized, remote viewers could be tasked on who issued both types of plates to the same party. This inquiry would remain secret, while perhaps unmasking a corrupt government official, or a mole in the host country's bureaucracy.

concrete tiers on one side... **Vehicle is moving very quickly, perhaps in the neighborhood of approximately 100 MPH** [162 km/h]**, maybe even a bit faster (in some spurts or straight-aways).**[5]

A view of their route along the Seine River. The red arrow
(top right corner) points the direct route to Fayed's apartment.

In my opinion, the driver was driving way beyond the speeds that would have been comfortable for the place and time. I believe he was well trained as a driver but not for the place or speed at which he was driving. I have a sense the driver was doing his damnedest to carry out the instructions of those he was carrying, but was operating at speeds and conditions that even he was never really trained to drive within. I think he was the professional here and was being egged on by the passengers.[6]

These sessions took place approximately ninety days before the release of the official fifty-two page report entitled, *Accident de Passage Souterrain de l'Alma. Paris Dimanche 31 Aout 1997, 0h25. Propostition d'Analyse Scientific et Technique. Synthese et Conclusions.* French Engineer Jean Pietri had been commissioned to write an engineering crash analysis, which went on to verify this earlier remote viewing material.

The distance from the first tunnel to the Pont de l'Alma tunnel is 1.2 kilometers (.75 mile). The speed limit is 30 mph (48km). It is here that published accounts differ. Apparently, three people witnessed four to six paparazzi motorcycles attempting to pull alongside the speeding Mercedes. Other accounts say the paparazzi were a quarter of a mile behind when the Mercedes entered the tunnel. In either event, it was all futile. Notified by telephone, reporters had already assembled at Dodi's apartment entrance, million-dollar picture in mind.

---

[5] The curve in the road is 480 meters [.3 miles] in front of the next tunnel, which provides an acceleration area. But with a subsequent curve and dip, it was not possible to negotiate that section of highway at high speed.

[6] McMoneagle was correct on this detail. Paul had attended special driving courses in Stuttgart, Germany from 1988 through 1993, receiving high marks, and Dodi knew this.

Evidential Details

McMoneagle – The Mercedes pulls out to pass a slower moving vehicle at a point in the road where the road ahead rises upward to a secondary overpass. Because of the rise in the road, the driver can't see on-coming traffic in time to avoid it, specifically at this speed.

The final report showed this was correct. French accident investigator Jean Pietri subsequently stated:

"To our surprise, we observed that the field of view is extremely limited. Passing cars disappear from sight well before they actually enter the tunnel because the descending road is obscured by a retaining wall. To the left the field of vision is blocked by a row of trees."[xxvii]

About 40 meters (44 yards) in front of the tunnel the Mercedes hit a gap in the pavement, which further destabilized control. As the car passed a white Fiat Uno at break neck speed Henri Paul saw another car dead ahead.

McMoneagle – I believe he sees an <u>on-coming</u> car which appears to be some kind of a black or dark green sedan. I want to say Citreon, but I'm really not sure. Probably a smaller two door car, two passengers; get a sense of dark green or green-black combination, which could mean a green car (body) **and black** (trim).

Mohammad Medjahdi was driving a Citroen BX with his girlfriend Souad in the tunnel ahead of the Fiat Uno.

McMoneagle – Dodi's last words - Have a fleeting sense that he [Paul] is being ordered to go faster and to do more erratic things, to avoid something. He is essentially being ordered to do what he is doing.

To avoid the <u>on-coming</u> traffic, the Mercedes driver swerves hard to the right and catches the small car he is passing [Fiat Uno] with his rear bumper. Car that was passed was hit. As a result, the Mercedes slews around left, just misses the <u>on-coming</u> car,[7] **which [it] has just passed, and the driver then begins to over-correct his steering.**

Months after these sessions, French engineers confirmed the Mercedes did nick the Fiat Uno and over corrected to the right. Some tail light/head light debris was found.[8] Engineers estimated that if the Mercedes was going 100 miles per hour the debris would have rolled sixteen meters (52.5 feet). That hit took place outside the tunnel and it is here the 18.9m (62ft) tire skid mark begins.

---

[7] McMoneagle was obviously inside looking through the Mercedes windshield. The use of "oncoming" describes the overtaking of cars. It does not refer to opposite direction traffic flow.

[8] The tail light pieces found in the tunnel belonged to a Fiat Uno manufactured between May 1983, and September 1989 by Seima Italiana. The white paint chips were called Bianco Corfu. When found, the car had been repainted.

Evidential Details

McMoneagle - The Mercedes hits the side to left slews across and hits the right, then swings back to the left, where it catches what appears to be a concrete tier or pier (#13 pillar) **of some kind, concrete pilasters, or some kind of upright** (steel reinforced) **concrete dividers, which it hits nearly head on.**

At 12:24 a.m., there was an explosion sound in the tunnel. The subsequent engineering report confirmed Henri Paul's last evasive actions was viewed correctly. Various eyewitnesses re-counted the collision. "Gaelle L., 40, a production assistant stated:

"At that moment, in the opposite lane, we saw a large car approaching at high speed. This car swerved to the left, then went back to the right and crashed into the wall with its horn blaring. I should note that in front of this car, there was another, smaller car."[xxviii]

McMoneagle - The Mercedes apparently nearly goes end over end rear to front, but doesn't quite make it [over the top], **instead spinning twice and winds up pointing back in the direction it was coming from.**

The car spinning 1 1/2 times remains unconfirmed. But there was enough inertia for the car to have spun 540 degrees when the rear wheels were off the ground. The impact was so hard that the forward roof area was crushed down to the level of the driver's knees. This is further substantiated by the fact Diana was found facing backward in the back seat, which would not have happened with a simple 180-degree turn. N*ewsweek Magazine* reported French police estimated the car had slowed down to 85 mph at the point of impact.[xxix]

The entire trip had taken about four minutes. Trevor Rees-Jones could only recall the Fiat Uno.

Rees-Jones: *"It seems to me there was one white car with a boot which opened at the back* [hatch back]*, and three doors but I don't remember anything else."*[xxx]

He did not leave the hospital until October 4 - thirty-four days later.

Aware Henri Paul did not have alcohol in his system we sought clarification to research about drugs in his blood stream.

McMoneagle - Substance review - I believe if the driver had drugs in his system, whatever kind they were, they were not there by his own hand. I have this sort of strange feeling that he was not deliberately drugged to hurt anyone, but maybe he was drugged to get the car stopped along the route for the "photographers" to get their shots. In other words, his control was tampered with by outside influ-

Evidential Details

ences. I don't think he was drunk, possibly drugged, but not drunk.

Here the research came full circle. The paparazzi had attempted to slow the Hotel Ritz airport shuttle vehicles earlier that afternoon on the drive from the airport. Once it was discovered, Henri Paul had been an informant for domestic as well as foreign intelligence services we went back to McMoneagle. Could the British government have been involved?

McMoneagle - My sense is that MI-5 (British Intelligence) **did not put the stuff in his drink. However, one might contemplate that if he [Paul] was willing to take money from foreign intelligence operatives, he most certainly would have been open to taking money from the Paparazzi. Maybe they were hedging their bets by having a small "drink" with him in the bar before he started driving.**

And what of the high carbon dioxide levels in Dodi's blood stream? Since this viewing, there were reports of a carbon monoxide suicide in Paris that night.

McMoneagle - You have to open your perception a little bit here. He did not have to have any evidence of CO_2 in his blood for them to find CO_2 in a blood sample. You only have to switch the samples at the hospital, the morgue, or the lab. Or, pay off the guy who is doing the tests. You could also conceivably rig the test equipment. Also, there are drugs, which will give a false reading as well.

His being drugged enough to cause the accident could be attributed to a drug delivered in coffee, tea, or a drink beforehand. It could also have been sprayed on the inner edge of his door handle (driver's side), painted on the steering wheel, or inside a pair of driving gloves. He could have been shot with a needle delivery system, or pricked his hand, finger, leg, or almost any part of his anatomy on a delivery system getting into or out of the car. It can even be filmed across the pages of a book or map that he might have used to check directions on.

If he had a normal medical condition, they could have used a drug, which reacts violently with the drugs he is already taking for the medical condition. In which case they would either get false readings, or evidence of his medicinal drug, plus some other known drug which would not have been viewed as culprit in the event, simply because no one recognized the possible expected reaction. You also have problems with drugs which are binary in nature and can be delivered in two sittings, so to speak, where the victim gets part A in the morning with breakfast, part B in the evening with dinner, both of which are enzymes and when mixed... cause everything from hallucinogenic behavior, to strokes.

Evidential Details

Next we turned to what Dodi and Diana where thinking.

McMoneagle - Back seat travelers - MAJOR PROBLEM: When I try to access others who might have been in the car, I get heavy [analytic] overlay and interference as relates to Diana's death in France. My head fills up with all kinds of motorcycles, and all kinds of news... that was being broadcast about the incident. I believe there were at least two others in this target car, but digging anything out of the overlay is completely impossible.

There is a sense from the people in the back seat that they want to be alone together, but again, I then get overwhelmed with all the Princess Diana stuff... and it all runs together. So, I can't begin to tell where [the] overlay begins and real data ends. Would prefer to say nothing.

It's rather interesting. I actually have not opened the envelope nor have a clue as to the real target here; but I am being overwhelmed with overlay which is self-generated. Must have been a lot of energy around the Princess Diana stuff. Better to just go no further with it. End of Session.

An abrupt stop, on a then well-known topic, due to analytic overlay. This is a graphic demonstration of the differences between military remote viewers, storefront psychics and hot lines. The media had been saturated with Princess Diana coverage in the period between the accident and this tasking. A psychic hot-liner would have been able to talk and bill without end about what they "saw". As one Operation Star Gate remote viewer commented, "There are many *"psychics"* who have taken this type of gibberish to a finely honed skill."[xxxi] But, when McMoneagle got to the Mercedes back seat, he stopped the session. In intelligence work when you are not sure of your viewing, you must say so. Any elaboration is unethical as in life and death situations, military viewers must stay grounded in the target's realities.

Analytic Overlay [AOL] is terminology within the Controlled Remote Viewing [CRV] protocols developed by Mr. Ingo Swann for the U.S. Military Intelligence Community at the Stanford Research Institute as they developed the nomenclature. AOL can generate bad data. So, can anything be done about it?

McMoneagle - Military research - There were a number of experiments which were run to examine whether or not a remote viewer can identify "AOL" while in session. We found that it could be rarely demonstrated. Most viewers are unable to tell (accurately or consistently) when something was AOL or when it wasn't, while in session.

Facts are; Evidence produced within labs suggests that no one methodology is capable of identifying and extinguishing AOL any

better than another over the long haul.

There have been significant runs of very low AOL or displays of almost no AOL which have been done by individual remote viewers. So, there are indications that some people might have a talent for producing less AOL than others. But it does not appear to be method driven since it doesn't hold up in testing across all remote viewers using the same method.

So, why should identifying AOL be important??? It is important because, while you are attempting to learn remote viewing (regardless of method), it makes you think about how and why you are "thinking" about something. It is meant to reduce the speed by which you automatically jump to a conclusion. It also supports the structure and keeps one within it (at least until one becomes proficient enough to no longer need it.)

After the impact, eyewitnesses saw a motorcycle 30 to 40 meters behind the Mercedes slow down to observe the accident and then accelerate away from the scene. At 12:26 a.m., the Paris Fire Department - Sapeurs-Pompiers Unit - received a cell phone call from a Gaelle who was in the tunnel. Within one minute another call went out to the "service d'aid medicale urgente" (SAMU) - a civilian emergency medical service.

In the wreck, Diana and bodyguard Trevor Rees-Jones were still alive. One eye witness said he heard a woman crying loudly. One of the paparazzi, Romuald Rat, indicated Diana was conscious. He claimed he told her to stay calm; that help was on the way.

Aftermath

Pandemonium broke out as the Press fought each other to get the new million dollar shot. One photographer leaned into the car to reposition Dodi's corpse for a posed picture. Someone else came with video equipment. Within five minutes, Police Officers Lion Gagliardone and Sebastien Dorzee plowed through the crowd to the car. The police report stated:

"*I observe the occupants in the vehicle are in a very grave state. I immediately repeat the call for aid and request police reinforcements, being unable to contain the photographers and aid the wounded.*"[xxxii]

Officer Dorzee: "*I finally got to the vehicle... The rear passenger* (Diana) *was also alive... She seemed to be in better shape* (than Rees-Jones). *However, blood flowed from her mouth and nose. There was a deep gash on her forehead. She murmured in English, but I didn't understand what she said. Perhaps 'My God!'*"[xxxiii]

Evidential Details

Ultimately, six paparazzi were held in connection with the frenzy in the tunnel. They were arrested on suspicion of involuntary homicide and failure to assist persons in danger. Excepting the 24-year-old Romuald Rat, 40 was the average age of those arrested. Twenty film rolls were confiscated providing police with the photographic evidence they needed to confirm each man's activities that night. Three paparazzi got away.

There are no Miranda rights in France, nor is there a right to call an attorney. French authorities can hold a suspect for forty-eight hours before the prisoner must be formally charged or set free. But it is certain Henri Paul did not have to be drunk or drugged to have had an accident at that speed.

The former Princess of Wales, Diana Spencer, arrived at the Hospital de la Pitie-Salpetriere at 2:00 a.m. She was pronounced dead at 4:00 a.m. It was then she attempted to contact her son William in Scotland. "William had had a difficult night sleep and had woken many times. That morning he had known, he said, that something awful was going to happen."[xxxiv] When he was told of his mother's death he said, "*I knew something was wrong. I kept waking up all night.*"[xxxv]

At 5:00 p.m. Prince Charles, 48, flew into Villacoublay military airfield outside Paris from Aberdeen, Scotland with Diana's sisters Sarah McCorquodale and Jane Fellows. "Diana's sisters spent most of the flight to Paris in tears. The Prince was controlled but clearly very shaken."[xxxvi] By 5:40 p.m. he was greeted at the hospital by the French President (1995-2007) and Mrs. Jacque Chirac. Charles was led into a room with his two now ex-sisters-in-law where Diana lay in a coffin. He asked to be alone with the body for a moment. When he came out his eyes were red. The accident was 368 days after the finalization of their divorce.

Diana's coffin, draped in the Royal Standard's yellow and maroon, was flown home by an honor guard in a British Royal Air Force BAe146 military aircraft to Northolt Air Force Base in England. She was then taken to the Chapel Royal at Saint James Place.

Undertaken by Levertons, her September 6 funeral was the largest in England since the death of former Prime Minister and Nobel Literature Prize winner Winston Churchill [1874-1965]. After the morning funeral, it was reported a million people lined the route as the body was taken from London's Westminster Abby. Different accounts estimated two to three billion people watched the day's events as the car traveled the seventy-five miles to Althorpe House. Late that afternoon her body was laid to rest on a 1,254 sq. meter (13,500 sqft) island called The Oval in a lake on the Spencer's ancestral grounds. The four hundred-year-old estate was then partially turned into a tourist attraction.

On September 9, 1997, the week after Diana was buried the Al-

Evidential Details

Fayed attorney filed civil law suits against the French periodicals *France-Dimanche* and *Paris-Match*. The complaint specified invasion of privacy with willful and wanton reckless endangerment when helicoptering "stalkerazzi" got too close over the Fayed's villa in St. Tropez. But, for the Hotel Ritz, the question became who bears responsibility for the accident? Before 1997 was out, the Fayed, Spencer, Rees-Jones and Paul families had all filed papers to be made civil parties to the investigation. Under French law, this allows them to investigate the case file and participate in any damage awards. And as for the Paparazzi's fate:

"In accordance with articles 175, 176 and 177 of the Code of Penal Procedure; The examining magistrates find that there is no case to answer in the case of the state versus the above named [Photographers]."[xxxvii]

In July, 2004 Queen Elizabeth II personally opened the Princess of Wales Memorial Fountain in the southwest corner of London's Hyde Park.

Then, in April 2008, after a three year investigation costing $7.3 million ($8.3 million/2016), a six month long British inquest report was released which included the testimony of 278 witnesses with more than 600 exhibits generating an 832 page report stating:

"Our conclusion is that, on the evidence available at this time, there was no conspiracy to murder any of the occupants of the car," Lord Stevens of Kirkwhelpington, who led the inquiry, told reporters as he presented his findings here. *"This was a tragic accident."*[xxxviii]

In September of 2012, the French magazine *Closer* published paparazzi photos of Diana's eldest son's wife Kate Middleton sunbathing topless while at the Queen's nephew Lord Linley's French chateau. A publically released statement on behalf of the Duke and Duchess said: *"The incident is reminiscent of the worst excesses of the press and paparazzi during the life of Diana, Princess of Wales, and all the more upsetting to The Duke and Duchess for being so."*

And as for the need to use remote viewing protocols:

McMoneagle - CRV (Controlled Remote Viewing) **is a "method" derived from a method the military used while attempting to "train" people to understand both protocol as well as what is going on in a remote viewer's head (such as processing or the lack thereof). It was also very specifically designed to "preclude" things from being done out of ignorance (during the RV session) that might impact on/or otherwise prevent the act of successful psychic functioning from taking place; in other words, insure that RV could be replicated and would work more times than not.**

Book I

What you are about to read is the data the Pentagon would have received if this event had been targeted in the interests of the People of the United States.

Evidential Details

Starting at the river side campgrounds east of Frederick, Maryland (middle right edge), this map details the parallel north-south mountain ranges, their passes, rivers, and each Southern General's destination (blue bars) as per the *Special Order*. Notice the Antietam Creek running south from just east of Hagerstown, MD (top border).

Evidential Details

The Greatest Mystery of the Civil War

Leading to America's Bloodiest Day, the Emancipation Proclamation and Europe's non-recognition of the Confederacy.

Solved

The causes of war are the same as the causes of competition among individuals: acquisitiveness, pugnacity, and pride; the desire for food, land, materials, fuels, mastery. The state has our instincts without our restraints.

Will & Ariel Durant

Evidential Details

It has been said success has a thousand fathers while failure is an orphan. But Historians have missed a curious exception to this rule as Confederate General Robert E. Lee implemented his bold plan to move the Civil War's carnage north in early September of 1862.

The American Civil War [1861-1865] put brother against brother in a struggle to resolve the nation's States Rights and slavery question. From Washington D.C. to Key West, Florida to El Paso, Texas, to Kansas City, Kansas, the Southern States wanted their own nation and fought a long hard war to realize their idea. And it brought innovation.

New non-lethal weapons emerged such as the first tactical use of telegraph, railroads and observation balloons. World War I (1914-1918) style trench works with obstructions were built. Iron clad vessels were launched making all the world's navies obsolete overnight. With new scoped and rifled musketry, cannon and artillery, revolvers, Gatling guns, field embalming, battlefield photography, and the world's most advanced prosthetics, this war is considered the first modern war. But for the Southerner, the "War Between the States" was considered a war for independence.

Summer – State of Virginia. In the midst of a near fatal military crisis, Southern General Robert E. Lee assumed command of the Army of Northern Virginia on June 1. By day 25, with a 72% numerically inferior force, he turned back the Federal advances at the gates of the Southern Capital Richmond, Virginia. That week a series of battles, known as the Seven Days campaign, has been compared to the fluidity of World War II battlefields. With his victories over Union Lieutenant General George McClellan, Lee swung his forces north to confront a second Union Army commanded by Major General John Pope [1822-1892]. In his last independent campaign Confederate Major General Thomas J. "Stonewall" Jackson opened the battle on August 9, at Cedar Mountain in Culpepper County.

Now, with a Southern Army that was 87% as large, Lee routed Pope's Federal forces at the Battle of Second Manassas. That campaign ended with Jackson slugging it out with Pope in a driving rainstorm at Chantilly Crossroads, on September 1, 1862.

After 90 days in command, Robert E. Lee had moved the battle lines from modern day east suburban Richmond, to the Potomac River northwest of Washington, D.C. Except for Norfolk, the State of Virginia had been virtually cleared of what was considered Federal occupation. Now, amid the Southern press clamoring for quick action to destroy the Union Army, Lee was weighing his options. If the Army moved north into Maryland, he hoped this border state might join the Confederacy. The South should then be able to recruit and hamper Washington D.C.'s westbound communications and supply. But after the conclusion of two major campaigns Lee had challenges.

Evidential Details

First, there was a need for military re-organization. General Lee added Wade Hampton's Cavalry and some reserve artillery under William Pendleton to his Army. He also added close to three Infantry Divisions in an effort to make up for the loss of approximately 9,000 men in the Second Manassas campaign.

Lee also had to settle command questions. After the recent combat losses, there were not enough Generals to go around. Colonels headed fifty-seven percent of Stonewall Jackson's fourteen Brigades. To ease this situation Generals Dick Garnett, John Bell Hood and A.P. Hill were released from arrest to resume field command.

Absent without leave and straggling was another problem. While considering the move into Maryland, upwards of 30,000 hungry men roaming northern Virginia were directed to meet at Winchester to be united into a cohesive fighting force and protect against being taken prisoner.

Shoddily manufactured boots, bad food and a quartermaster who could not sufficiently supply the Army aggravated the situation. As Confederate Major General Daniel Harvey Hill wrote: *"The order excusing barefooted men from marching into Maryland had sent thousands to the rear."*[xxxix] Soldiers were constantly falling out due to bad nutrition resulting in "GI" symptoms. Compounding the problem was that many young officers, whose average age was now in the early 30's, simply did not have experience keeping irregular columns of soldiers closed.

And finally, the Confederate High Command was plagued with injuries. General James Longstreet was unable to wear a boot due to a painful foot blister. Generals Jackson and Lee himself had both been involved in horse accidents. Jackson was thrown from a new horse he received from a pro-Confederate Marylander when his horse went missing. And General Lee's hands were in splints from a fall while trying to restrain his horse Traveller. He was carried into Maryland in an ambulance.

Lee wrote to Confederate President Jefferson Davis:

"The Army is not properly equipped for an invasion of an enemy's territory. It lacks much of the material of war, is feeble in transportation, the animals being much reduced, and the men are poorly provided with clothes, and in thousands of instances are destitute of shoes."[xl]

To counter this Lee authorized the Quartermaster to buy cornfields, orchards and wooden fences for firewood. In his memoirs, Confederate General John Bell Hood, recalled:

"My troops, at this period, were sorely in need of shoes, clothing and food. We had had issued to us no meat for several days, and little or no bread; the men had been forced to subsist principally on green corn and green apples.

Evidential Details

Nevertheless, they were in high spirits and defiant, as we contended with the advance guard of McClellan..."[xli]

Alfred R. Waud, September 1862, Library of Congress
Union observers take shots as the Confederate Calvary moves
inbound (northerly) across the Potomac River at different locations.

Rather than laying siege to Washington, Lee decided to try and draw the Union Army out into the open by moving northwest across the Potomac River. As his Army of Northern Virginia was being reshaped, Lee was analyzing an ambitious plan to split his forces five ways in the face of an enemy twice his size.

On Thursday September 4, Confederate soldiers started to cross the Potomac River up from Leesburg, Virginia at White's Ford. The passage of 45,000 men required approximately three days. "There was no one to stop them on the Northern shore; only wide-eyed civilians looked at the most ragged, dirty and profane men they could remember. Leighton Parks, a Maryland boy of twelve, saw them as 'a hungry set of wolves,' but he admired the horsemanship of (Calvary General J.E.B.) Stuart's troopers;"[xlii]

While history records troop jubilation upon crossing the river, in some towns what is not recorded is that during the next few days attitudes changed. The men understood they were outnumbered in enemy territory and that their supply lines were extended. Their crossing of a major river made timely supply an open question. And their now compromised ability to maintain surprise was a major Southern apprehension.

Author
Modern day White's Ferry facing southeast. The four minute trip across the Potomac River allows historians to interpret Confederate troops moving into Maryland (top left) from Virginia.

Once in Maryland, the Confederate General Staff found their reception muted. "A staff officer recorded: *The inhabitants of Maryland whom we met along the road...did not greet us quite so cordially as we had expected...*"[xliii9] After the Southern troops had gone into camp, 135 years later Joseph McMoneagle sat in front of a double blind targeting envelope to acquire a time and place coordinate.

McMoneagle - Somewhere in the Northeast. My very first impression is that of circles inside of circles. Usually, for me anyway, this signifies duplicity or deceit. I also get a sense that this wasn't the only time such deceit was used or attempted during a specified period of time. I have a sense that it was lost near to, or on the edge of, a major city, somewhere Northwest of Washington D.C. perhaps.

This is a Confederate camp. I get a sense they are preparing for a large battle, the clashing of nearly two complete armies. They are bringing so many troops into the area, they are nervous that (their) troop movements will be known, or that spies might be in the area. A major battle is only a few days away and has something to do with a small town with flanking... positions that run parallel to a road.

The small town is Sharpsburg, Maryland. The parallel road is the Hagerstown Turnpike.

---

[9] An Adjutant-General's report from Washington DC., dated November 9, 1880, stated Maryland furnished 46,638 Union troops; Southern enlistment's from the 1862 Maryland Campaign are estimated at 200.

Evidential Details

General Lee's plan was to draw Federal forces out of the heavily fortified Washington D.C. He would then strike General McClellan somewhere in western Maryland with a rested, re-organized and re-equipped army via the Shenandoah Valley. But before he could do this, he needed to reduce the Federal commands at Harpers Ferry and Martinsburg in modern day West Virginia,[10] while his army lay screened behind the Catoctin and South Mountain ranges.

Lee finalized his plans on Tuesday, September 9. The Army of Northern Virginia, previously of smaller independent commands, was to coordinate across two rivers to surround a division of 12,500 Union infantrymen accompanied by 1,500 cavalry. The target, Harpers Ferry, in what was the State of Virginia, had already changed hands twice. His strategy, outlined in *Special Order 191*, dispatched 26 of the Army's 40 brigades twenty-five miles apart in the face of the Union Army's four Corps. As a result, there was no time for a siege; Harpers Ferry had to be taken outright. General Thomas J. "Stonewall" Jackson was assigned this task.

With a ~45,000 vs. 87,000 troop strength inferiority, Lee's orders were bold. He was counting on the newly restored Union General George McClellan's cautiousness. Lee knew that dividing his forces, in the face of almost 2 to 1 odds is how armies are "defeated in detail." In military circles, this force separation is known as a violation of Concentration of Mass. However, once decided upon, it is vitally important to maintain the principle of Security. Should this be compromised, the principle of Surprise is violated. Surprise was the critical component of the Confederate plan to make his Maryland campaign a success. Once Surprise is compromised by a lack of Security, Maneuver is reduced. Should a numerically superior enemy learn about smaller divided enemy forces throughout history the army, and usually the cause, is lost.

McMoneagle - I believe within two, possibly three days' time, they were moving to join a battle... This was a major battle that involved at least four divisions of men, maybe more, spread across a battle line at least ten miles wide and six to ten miles wide...

The town of Harpers Ferry sits at the confluence of the Shenandoah and Potomac Rivers. Once Lee was north of the Potomac, the elimination of this Federal garrison became essential to maintain a Southern line of communication. After consultations with his Generals in Frederick, Mary-

---

[10] Virginia's western counties gathered in Wheeling to nullify Richmond's secession act of June 11, 1861. In April 1862, a new constitution was drafted and a separate Governor, Francis H. Pierpont, appointed. On April 20, 1863, President Lincoln proclaimed the State of West Virginia, to be effective in 60 days, making it the 35th State. The capital of Charleston was not announced until 1885.

Evidential Details

land, Lee's *Special Order 191* was issued indicating where each commander was to deploy for the week. Paraphrased, the orders specified:

- General Thomas J. Jackson [1824-1863] was to seize the Baltimore & Ohio Railroad and to drive the Martinsburg garrison (2,500 men) south to Harpers Ferry. Then on to Harpers Ferry, attacking by land from Bolivar Heights in today's West Virginia. Jackson's men would have to march and fight over fifty-one miles in two days to be there on the third.
- General Lafayette McLaws [1821-1897] was to attack Harpers Ferry from Maryland Heights on the Maryland side of the Potomac River. He was to report to Jackson.
- General James Walker [1821-1893] was ordered to attack Harpers Ferry from Loudon Heights across the Shenandoah River from Virginia. He was to report to Jackson.
- General James Longstreet [1821-1904] was to occupy Hagerstown, Maryland and remain in reserve.
- General Daniel Harvey Hill [1821-1889] was ordered to bring up the rear moving to Boonesboro, Maryland, with the cannon and supply trains.

As the last division to cross, Confederate Major General D.H. Hill's men went into bivouac east southeast of Frederick, Maryland on the Monocracy River. Once drawn up, General Lee sent his orders via standard military courier confident he would retain the advantage of Surprise. As ordered, Southern arms moved the next morning separating across Western Maryland.

McMoneagle – I have a strong feeling of anxiety within the camp. I think these men know they are outnumbered and are nervous about having crossed a river and then camping in a place that essentially leaves it at their back. Very little sound in the camp - - like they are trying not to make any/or as little noise as possible. The weather is cool at night, but somewhat warm during the day - maybe the beginning of the Fall? At least that's what the weather feels like.

Wood smoke in the air. Some food smells. Smells like morning food versus later day food. Heavy mist in the air, maybe ground fog. Damp and cool [near high 60's F]. Sounds of breaking camp. Lots of muffled sounds, as though everyone is trying not to make any noise; Horses being saddled, traces being hooked up on wagons. Can hear orders being given in the distance, as men are marched away.

On the move, one Southern General recalled:

<u>D.H. Hill</u>: *The Confederates, with more than half of Lee's Army at Harpers Ferry, distant march of two days, and with the remainder divided into two parts, thirteen miles from each other, were in good condition to be beaten in detail, scattered and captured"*[xliv]

Evidential Details

McMoneagle - The Confederate soldiers, who were camped near the trees where the packet was found, dismantled their camp there and were out of the area within two to three hours of the man leaving who had actually lost the packet. It was also lost early in the war.[11] **Either just prior to** (Antietam) **or... following a major battle** (Second Manassas). **Once the camp was packed up and loaded on wagons and mules, they moved the camp in what feels like a Northeast... direction, towards a river** (to the Monocracy River's Ford).

The Southern population was impressed with Robert E. Lee. "There was already talk of invading the North to teach the Yankee aggressors a lesson. The end of the war seemed near in these first days of September, 1862."[xlv] As D.H. Hill's division disappeared west through Frederick, M.D. and up into the mountains, the Confederates now held the high ground. Screened by two mountain ranges, and a superb Calvary, the undefeated Robert E. Lee led, man for man, the toughest and most dedicated veteran soldiers ever deployed in the Americas. Now the Rebels had slipped away somewhere northwest of Washington D.C. And from the mountain tops they could monitor Federal activity.

* * *

Ever the dramatic, Union Lieutenant General George Brinton McClellan penned a letter to his wife Mary Ellen from his office in Washington D.C. at just after 11:00 a.m. on the morning of September 5, 1862. "...*again I have been called upon to save the country - the case is desperate... - Truly God is trying me in the fire...*"[xlvi]

General McClellan had just been directed by President Abraham Lincoln to resume Eastern Theater Army command the day after the Confederates started their move into Maryland. But the 36-year-old was uncertain how to manage in the face of his recent week long military reversals around Richmond, Virginia.

Though in command of a larger and better equipped fighting force, McClellan worried about what Robert E. Lee would do next. But convinced he was history's "Man of Destiny" called to save the Union, McClellan continued his bold offensive measures correspondence with President Lincoln, while he paced his office.

A veteran Confederate army was on the move and the populace was uneasy. Alarmist fears of a Southern invasion all the way to Baltimore, Philadelphia and even New York were voiced. With a confident enemy

---

[11] The packet was lost in the eighteenth month of a forty-eight month war.

Evidential Details

moving toward the Pennsylvania border, a stunned Governor Andrew G. Curtin became extremely concerned about Southern intentions.

Aside from not knowing where the enemy was, McClellan also had organizational problems. First, he had to merge his defeated Richmond (Peninsula) Campaign forces with a thoroughly demoralized Union Army of Virginia after their defeat at Second Manassas. Additionally, he had to train, equip and organize no fewer than 35 new regiments of 500 men each. This had to be done in extreme haste and it was a credit to McClellan he organized as quickly as he did.

But McClellan's biggest problem was intelligence gathering. He was up against Western Maryland's topography of Parr's Ridge and the Catoctin mountain ranges. This array of parallel Appalachian hills hampered horse mounted intelligence gathering. These responsibilities had been recently delegated to Cavalry Brigadier General Alfred Pleasonton [1824-1897]. Hard working and a fighter, Pleasonton was nonetheless unable to penetrate the Rebel Cavalry screen.

Having lost the initiative again, McClellan needed information in three critical areas: the Rebel army's whereabouts; General Lee's intentions; enemy numbers. As he stewed, he became concerned about the implications of a misstep leading to another military disaster. Having taken Robert E. Lee's repeated beatings with smaller forces, he fretted about:

"*...a gigantic rebel army*" worrying that, "*Every other consideration should yield to this; and if we defeat the army now arrayed before us, the rebellion is crushed. But if we should be so unfortunate as to meet with defeat, our country is at their mercy.*"[xlvii]

Consider his personal drama. With a confident and undefeated Confederate Army screened and on the move somewhere northwest of Washington D.C. the United States, and the Lincoln Administration's, future was on the line. On the other hand, as far as the President was concerned, it was time Theater Commander McClellan issue the orders to put this rebellion down and restore the Union.

McMoneagle - McClellan - I would guess that he was one of the top four or five Union Generals. I have a sense that he eventually got into trouble as a result of his 'fear of deceit -- or caution' whichever way you want to look at it. He probably wasn't a very decisive person. Competent overall, but not very aggressive. I also have a distinct feeling or sense that this particular Union commander was particularly cautious anyway. Always looking for deceit, duplicity, or manipulation where there was none to be found. I get a strong sense the Union General was a real screw up in that regard - as we say in the military -

Evidential Details

Mathew Brady or assistant - The National Archives
Union Theater Commander General George McClellan [1826-1885] Commander of the Army of the Potomac and the Democratic Party's 1864 Presidential candidate against the incumbent Abraham Lincoln.

Evidential Details

Julian Vannerson, 1863. Library of Congress
Confederate Commander Robert E. Lee [1807-1870] of the Army of Northern Virginia.

a man of no vision. Gutless.

"In the Peninsula (campaign) Lee had out generaled McClellan in large part through his understanding of the personality...of the Commander."[xlviii] Psychologically, for McClellan, staving off defeat would be victory. So, when one of Lee's top secret orders packets went missing, both armies became engaged in a desperate struggle that would determine the timing of the elimination of slavery in the United States.

Evidential Details

Cautious, General McClelland did order troops forward to the unincorporated community of Ijamsville, Maryland seven miles east southeast of Frederick, M.D. In 1831, one of the town founders, Plummer Ijams II, had granted a right of way to the Baltimore and Ohio Railroad to construct a route through his town as long as they agreed to build a depot. It was on the grounds, close to that right of way, that the Union's XII Corps bivouacked on Friday night the 12th.

* * *

On Saturday morning September 13, Union 12th Corps had orders to advance from Ijamsville northwest along what is today Reich's Ford Road east of Frederick. As the first Union men to move into the area since the Rebel departure, Federal scouts were detailed out to General D.H. Hill's old campground before dawn.

McMoneagle - Union scouting - Some men were actually sent to check out the old (Confederate) camp area. These scouts or outriders were deliberately sent to the old encampment in order to collect as much intelligence as they could about strength, health and welfare of the enemy. They did this to determine approximately how many men were in the camp, how many horses, to look for garbage burial sites to see how well the men were eating, count wagon wheel ruts - - to estimate cannon, etc; General intelligence collection on the enemy.

It was during this mission that Union scouts found an "envelop" next to a tree. Inside was General Lee's *Special Order 191*. This would determine the outcome of Lee's whole Maryland campaign. When, where, how and why the packet was found have been historical controversies ever since.

As the mystery has been recounted, General Lee's dispatch was found in different places in different ways. For instance, in *Stonewall - A Biography of General Thomas J. Jackson*, author Byron Farwell described the event:

> "Private Barton Warren Mitchell of Company F, perhaps <u>looking for some firewood</u>, found the envelope which to his delight, contained three cigars. He at once showed his find to First Sergeant John McKnight Bloss ...and they were astonished to see that it also had Confederate orders... With astonishing rapidity the orders were passed up the chain of command, from company commander Captain Peter Kopp, to regimental commander Colonel Silas Colgrove, to the division headquarters of Brigadier General Alpheus Starkey Williams..."[xlix]

But later, Colonel Colgrove stated he received the packet directly from First Sergeant Bloss, not Captain Kopp. So in an unusual wartime dev-

Evidential Details

Google Map Data 2011 Google Sanborn

In motion from Rockville, Maryland (lower right corner). The blue line shows the Twelfth Corps march to confront Confederate forces northwest of Washington D.C.

elopment, the Lieutenant, Captain and Major's ranks were bypassed. This reporting violation was an indication of Bloss's concern.

Evidential Details

Sergeant Bloss's scouting team worked north along the Monocracy River to meet up with the advancing infantrymen at Crum's Ford. The memoire of Private Edmund R. Brown, 17, recounted their march along Reich's Road to cross Crum's Ford on their way to Frederick, M.D.

"On the 13th we moved by the direct road to Frederick." "There being no bridge over the Monocracy, on this road, we forded the stream." "But with skirmishers still in our front <u>we moved on</u> (west) and finally halted in a <u>clover field</u>, adjoining the city (Frederick) on the south."[li]

In the Pulitzer Prize winning *Landscape Turned Red – The Battle of Antietam*, author Stephen Sears recounted the occasion:

"...The Indiana boys found a comparatively <u>unspoiled section of meadow along side a rail fence</u> and settled down to boil their coffee and relax. Sergeant John M Bloss and Corporal Barton W. Mitchell of company F were <u>chatting idly</u> when Mitchell noticed a bulky envelope in the <u>tall grass</u> nearby and picked it up. Inside was a <u>sheet of paper</u> wrapped around three cigars."[li]

In *The Secret War for the Union*, Edwin Fishel wrote:

"McClellan was referring to the greatest intelligence find of the war --- a copy of Special Orders No. 191 of the Army of Northern Virginia. Wrapped around three cigars ...the order was found by Corporal Barton W. Mitchell, [12] a soldier in his forties, when his regiment, the 27th Indiana Infantry, camped <u>in a clover field at Frederick</u> that morning. Saturday, September 13."[lii]

In *Stonewall Jackson - Portrait of a Soldier*, author John Bowers speculated:

"...a Federal soldier had noticed a package lying in the <u>middle of the road</u>. It had dropped from the <u>back pocket of a Confederate Officer</u>. It was Special Order 191 wrapped around a pack of fine cigars."[liii]

In *The Civil War Papers of George B. McClellan*, Editor Stephen W. Sears stated:

"The copy of his operational plan (was) lost by a <u>Confederate courier</u>..."[liv]

So, did an Officer, a courier, or a soldier drop the packet? Was it found at noon while Union soldiers were looking for firewood? Or, were they

---

[12] The man that found the orders, Corpora Bartonl Mitchell, was severely wounded at the Battle of Antietam a week later and spent the next eight months in a hospital. He died from war wounds three years after the war in Bartholomew, Indiana. After some efforts, his wife went without a war pension.

Evidential Details

Courtesy Global Geo Eye, Commonwealth of Virginia, U.S. Geological Survey, Map Data ©2012 Google

The blue line shows Twelth Corps 4.5 mile morning march. The 27th Indiana was on the point. The beige arrows show where Sergeant Bloss's scouts rode to inspect the former Confederate campground. The star (left edge) shows the Confederate officer's tent location.

Evidential Details

2012 Europa Technologies; 2012 Google; Image U.S. Geological Survey

Marching left to right at less than 4 mph (6.4km). History's first terrain analysis demonstrates why it took all morning for the 27th Indiana to cover 4.5 miles (7.2k). The men had to march against a 3.1% average slope up to a 19.6% grade at the peak of a 523 (159.4m) foot hill. On the west side, they had a 4% average downhill with a 20.2% maximum slope. It slowed the Union advance that morning.

idly boiling coffee and chatting by a rail fence? Was the packet found in short clover, tall meadow grass, or in the middle of the road? For the first time the true historical scenario is revealed

McMoneagle - Almost dark. Feels like it is going to rain; overcast and slight wind. Absolutely silent. No talking, just the sounds of a horse coughing, or hoof striking the ground, now and then. No more than twelve men on horses, standing around, while a man is going through the packet to see what he's found. Man who found the packet has a civilian shirt on, so there is no rank. I believe they are all dressed as civilians, although I have a sense they are scouts for a Union unit somewhere to the northeast or east-northeast. They found the packet under a tree near where the camp had been...

The lost object itself is cream or buff colored. Approximately 6 - 8 inches long; 3.5 to 4 inches wide; 1 to 1.5 inches thick. It may be made of cloth or skin, my guess being the latter as there are specific kinds of folds in it, which are complicated and deliberate -- something akin to origami [intricate folds]. There is paper inside wrapped around something soft. The object(s) I know now to be cigars, makes perfect sense. I was translating them as hotdogs, which of course didn't exist back then. A real problem for me. The exterior wrapping was a soft skin, probably deer hide which was rolled over and tied shut. I believe the contents were further wrapped in papers that were important to the man who owned the cigars.

The lost object was actually about palm size. It was found at the base of a small tree, where it had apparently been dropped or left on the ground. The pouch originally belonged to the Confederacy.

When found, it was found by Union soldiers. It was probably In-

Evidential Details

McMoneagle RV Art – Evidential Details ©1997
RV drawing of the Special Orders packet, showing cigar placement. The upper right notes read: **"Sketches of pouch and how it worked; constructed of deer skin. Supple and essentially water proof."**

Evidential Details

dianans. So, **if it was found by soldiers from an Indiana outfit** (27th Indiana; Gordon's Brigade; 1st Division, 12th Corp), **then it was found by Union soldiers. Probably scouts or flank riders -- that is men who... scouted ahead or to the side of a division or larger...**

McMoneagle RV Art - Evidential Details ©1997

General D.H. Hill's 1862 Monocracy River Bivouac

Top right the notes read: **Rolling hills in fenced but open country; sporadic trees; mostly farm land**. Notice McMoneagle's sense of stratification including the geographic term "hill" inside the red square.

Evidential Details

U.S. Geological Survey; Image 2012 Terrametrics; ©2012 Google Earth

From 1185 feet, this map shows the bend in the Monocracy River that matches McMoneagle's map. As the scouts left the road for the vacated camp, this may be how they approached (**blue arrows**). The Confederate Officers departed north-northeast around the river's bend up to Crum's Ford.

Evidential Details

Brigadier General A. S. Williams [1810-1878] was Union XII Corp's temporary commander pending Major General Joseph K. F. Mansfield's arrival. He received the packet. But what emerged from these remote viewing sessions was a new time line regarding exactly when Union scouts entered D .H. Hill's former campground and discovered *Special Order 191*. We discovered it was retrieved at dawn, but was reported to have been found at about 11:00 a.m. just as Colonel Colgrove arrived on the scene. As sometimes happens in remote viewing, new information results in a reinterpretation of what have been established historical facts.

Union Scout Commander – First Sergeant John M. Bloss

After the rough march, the 27th Indiana Volunteers started to arrive at the Monocracy River before noon. Just after the Colonel arrived, First Sergeant John Bloss handed him the mysterious packet. But, with this new time line, there is an approximate six hour difference between when the men claimed they found the packet, and McMoneagle's before dawn findings. So we decided to see if there were any evidential details that could clear up the discrepancy.

In the Civil War, scouting parties located enemy positions and reported back on enemy camp conditions. This had to be done before occupying troop traffic disturbed the grounds. As it turned out, the packet was found at what was the Confederate Officer's hitching tree area on a rise in the ground. As the Union troops searched in "no man's land", it would make sense a scouting party would simply wait for the troop's arrival. But, in order to believe history, one must be ready to accept that the scouting party looked everywhere except the rise with the tree, until six hours of daylight - dawn to 11:00 a.m. had passed. Then, in an even greater leap of faith, you must believe the men found the packet just as the Colonel arrived.

Sergeant Bloss's scouts had been detailed out to inspect a vacated Confederate camp. The First Sergeant had to complete his job, with a squad of men, within a specific time frame. It is not known if Bloss ever received written orders. But as per standard procedure, his men scouted the campground and recorded anything important. They then moved north and stood as river pickets around Crum Ford. McMoneagle was contacted by telephone for clarification on his dawn vs. the midday historical version. He replied:

Evidential Details

U.S. Geological Survey; Image C 2012 Terrametrics; © 2012 Google Earth

From 760 feet, today's rendezvous area. The orange arrow is Sergeant Bloss's scouting party moving north to rest along the road that morning. The **blue arrows** are the 27th Indiana starting to arrive from Ijamsville at approximately 11:00 a.m. (**upper right**). Exactly where Colonel Colgrove received Sergeant Bloss is unknown. Clearly, the Confederate Officer's former tent grounds were too far from the road for the orders to have *"just been found"* when the Coronel arrived. This accounts for why the men were relaxing as the advance elements of Company C started to arrive.

Evidential Details

McMoneagle - I don't believe that for a minute. The scouts found the packet early in the morning but had other duties before their assignment would have been completed. They scouted the whole area and then waited until the Colonel had moved in and started pitching his tent.

Where this mysterious package was concerned there were no orders. With his limited manpower, Sergeant Bloss chose not to reduce his numbers to deliver a questionable packet. Let an officer make the decision around noon. He simply held it and waited for the first officer he saw. As he looked the orders over, one cigar was probably smoked.

Interestingly, this historical revision clarifies the officer's conduct. If the scouts had the packet all morning, they would have had the ability to refer it to Colonel Colgrove immediately upon his arrival. Bloss must have considered it important because he ignored chain of command regulations and walked over to the Colonel when he arrived. We decided to check if the obscure Colonel Colgrove had ever made a statement about this packet.

Remarkably, in a letter written almost a quarter of a century later, it was clear in Silas Colgrove's mind how quickly he received the package. In a letter dated June 2, 1886, he recalled the day's events:

<u>Colonel Colgrove</u>: "*We stacked arms on the same ground that had been occupied by General D.H. Hill's division...*" Colgrove's next statement remained unacknowledged by historians at the time of this research.

<u>Colonel Colgrove</u>: "*Within a very few minutes after halting, the order was brought to me by First Sergeant John M. Bloss and Private* (Corporal) *B.W. Mitchell...*"[lv]

Almost twenty-four years later Colgrove emphasized the delivery's promptness. The "*within a very few minutes*" time frame suggests Sergeant Bloss brought the package upon the Colonel's arrival. Considering the packet important, it took Bloss just a few minutes to walk across the field.

One does not have to be a scholar to question a perfect timing packet discovery dovetailing with the Colonel's riding into the area. But this is what was reported, as the scouts were trapped. To claim to have overlooked the packet all morning, in broad daylight, would have been extreme scouting negligence in the face of the enemy. On the other hand, if genuine, no one would want to be accused of sitting on intelligence like this for half a day. So for the record, Colonel Colgrove thought it best to report they had just found it. Two and one half decades later, the Colonel emphasized there had been no foot dragging where he was concerned.

<u>Colonel Colgrove</u>: "*I immediately took the order to...headquarters, and delivered it to Colonel S.E. Pittman, General Williams adjutant-general.*"

Evidential Details

The officer receiving the packet from Sergeant Bloss was Union Colonel Silas Colgrove of the 27th Indiana, shown here in Brigadier Generals uniform. Aware of what had happened, he "*immediately*" forwarded the packet to General Williams.

McMoneagle – General William's Field Tent - I believe the packet was delivered to the Divisional Headquarters for the Union. There were four pickets, or guards, outside the tent at each corner, approximately twenty to twenty-five paces away. There were other officers within 45 to 60 paces of the tent, in a row of tents. It was taken to the General's tent and he opened it inside. There were two other people present inside the tent besides the General, his Aide - and his second in command - a Colonel. The papers in the packet were brought to the General's attention by the officer in charge. He was then dismissed from the tent.

After reviewing the document, General Williams was not sure what to make of it. Here was the information the Federals could not get. Williams was holding Lee's secret Maryland campaign orders as if he was a Confederate General himself. But were they genuine? What happened next ranks as one of military history's most astonishing coincidences.

Before the war General Williams, Colonel Pittman, and since June 2, General Lee's Chief of Staff and Acting Adjutant, now a Confederate Colonel, Robert Hall Chilton, had all worked together in Detroit, Michigan. Chilton had been Michigan's Army Paymaster since July, 1854. Pittman had been a railroad official who did banking business through Chilton. Due to repeated payroll transactions, Pittman was able to identify Chilton's signature as authentic on the spot in the tent. He was likely the only soldier in the Union Army familiar enough with Chilton's autograph to make an immediate identification. His considered opinion had an abrupt psychological impact on General Williams as he weighed the proper response.

Michigan's Brigadier General Alpheus Starkey Williams (seated center) and staff.

McMoneagle - These papers contained drawings and writing done with a wooden and metal tipped pen. They described a ground layout, which essentially included some kind of a main road, which crossed a main river (Potomac) **and ran through a small town** (Harpers Ferry). **Opposite the town was also a large creek** (Shenandoah River in September) **that flowed into the river as well. There were specific orders that were written out that accompanied this drawing, showing the placement of troops and equipment, as well as the primary or overall instructions as to what was intended to be accomplished. It is possible that the papers were copied.**

They were. Stonewall Jackson had provided a second copy to Daniel Harvey Hill who, before Lee's army's reorganization, had reported to Jackson.

But consider the probabilities against instant recognition. In a scenario that no fiction writer would attempt, there was about a one in 159,000 chance that any particular Union soldier, in the Eastern Theater, would happen upon the packet that day (87,000 men around Rockville,

Evidential Details

Maryland; 72,000 men in Washington D.C.). And across the scores of square miles, the "location" requirement was mathematically complicated by a fluidity variable because the entire XII Corps was in motion.

Then there was the officer's rank requirement to be in the General's tent. Next, there was the extremely narrow ten minute time window. Once the orders were forwarded to headquarters, there would be no opportunity to see them again. Pitman's opportunity to identify the signature existed only at the moment Silas Colgrove arrived at General William's tent.

There was also the personnel substitution variable. Chilton's handwriting was spotted because he was substituting for Lee's Adjutant Walter Taylor. And unlike Taylor, Chilton, 47, did not keep up the courier log to confirm if a signed receipt had been returned. Mixed together the probabilities against confirmation, at the point of decision, become nearly impossible to calculate.[13]

Because of the ramifications of finding the Special Order, what happened inside General William's tent has always been of unobtainable interest to Civil War buffs; an encounter forever lost. The packet contained a dispatch marked Confidential. Dated September 9, it was entitled: *"Headquarters, Army of Northern Virginia, S.O. 191. Official, R.H. Chilton, A.A.G."*. This order was addressed to Confederate Major General Daniel Harvey Hill.

McMoneagle – In William's Tent - The General and the Colonel (Colgrove) were the only ones to discuss the contents, and both were decidedly wary of the information contained within the paper[s]. They both felt that it was a Confederate ruse. The Colonel advised <u>not</u> to share knowledge of the papers with higher headquarters, but the General felt the information should be known. He forwarded it with a personal note that recommended it be taken with mistrust.

Silas Colgrove's behavior suggests he was aware of the scout's delay. First, he pointed out his prompt packet receipt. Then he mentioned his immediate delivery to Williams. But more importantly, he then recommended his commanding Officer, "**not to share knowledge of the papers with higher headquarters**." This is defensive behavior regarding the war's most important piece of intelligence. Why should Colgrove care what the General did? It was because he had his men to protect.

Consider the alternatives. If Headquarters thought this information

---

[13] Robert Hall Chilton [1815-1879] has been accused of the orders loss. As Lee's Acting Adjutant, the theory is that, a traitor, he enlisted a courier to drop the packet where it was certain to be found. The allegation's basis is Chilton's 1863 mishandling of Confederate General Jubal Early's discretionary retreat order at the Battle of Chancellorsville which could have caused a disaster for Confederate arms.

Evidential Details

genuine, it should be what an Officer would want his unit to take credit for. But on the other hand, if Colgrove was aware that the scouts sat on the orders, he had every reason to believe he had been handed the proverbial "cans of worms." If genuine, there was reason to fear an Army Inquiry surrounding the circumstances of how, when, where and by whom the packet had been discovered. Nobody would want to admit his men failed to take action to bring this information forward for half a day.

McMoneagle – In the case of this target, it was not only something that was lost, but it was also found. I believe both the 'losing of something' as well as the 'finding of something' was honestly done. It was accidentally left in a place that was commonly used or common to use by both the Union as well as the Confederacy...

The contents are critically important for some reason. I believe the documents were passed to a divisional commander who probably passed them to a ranking General in the Union Army (McClellan). **This is probably a large Union force -- Army size.**

After getting the orders packet in a very short time, and taking it immediately to Williams' tent, Colgrove emphasized:

Colonel Colgrove: *"It was at once taken to General McClellan's headquarters by Colonel Pittman."*[lvi]

In his note to Headquarters, Williams made sure to mention a corporal found the orders.

General William's Note: *"I enclose a Special Order of General Lee commanding Rebel Forces which was found on the field where my corps is encamped. It is a document of interest & is also thought genuine. The document was found by a corporal of the 27 Ind. Rgt, Col. Colgrove, Gordon's Brigade."*[lvii]

Normally, a General would want to come forward with "look what my outfit found" as a morale builder after a summer of defeats. Maybe the Corporal and the Sergeant should get leave or an extra stripe for meritorious conduct. The whole regiment could take pride in having been the ones to discover General Lee's battle plans. According to the Commander in Chief:

General McClellan: *"Whoever found the order in question and transmitted it to the headquarters showed intelligence and deserved marked reward, for he rendered an infinite service."*[lviii]

But even though he wrote an autobiography, A.S. Williams never penned or spoke publically about the lost orders. Remarkably, XII Corp. wanted the whole matter dropped and recognition for a job well done was never mentioned - even after the orders were verified to have been genuine.

McMoneagle - I still keep getting circles within circles, which usually indicates deceit or intelligence mumbo-jumbo... It's as if he is

deliberately hiding. So, there is a feeling of duplicity. There is something very 'spooky' or 'undercover' about this object. An object of intelligence or intelligence derived.

The National Archive

A Union General's field tent. One can image two officers standing, looking at the lost orders packet. Here President Lincoln confers with General McClelland after the Battle of Antietam. McClellan was subsequently relieved of command for failure to pursue in force as the Confederates returned to Virginia.

This isn't the first time, nor will it be the last time, that something true becomes something false, something known becomes

Evidential Details

something unknown, or that simple acts are twisted through perhaps (Colgrove's) **disinformation.**

It now appears the "fatherless" Lost Orders were in Union hands the entire morning. The behavior indicates the Coronel knew the orders had been sat on. One can imagine his chagrin when he realized Colonel Pittman's signature identification meant any further effort to prevent the orders from moving up the ladder would seem suspicious. This packet was so important that:

Colonel Colgrove: "...*had it not been for the finding of the lost order, the battle of South Mountain, and probably that of Antietam, would not have been fought.*"[lix]

And what about General Williams?

McMoneagle - I have a sense that he did not do well physically. ...my sense is that he did not suffer from war wounds or anything like that, but was generally subject to quite a bit of sickness in his years during the war as well as immediately following it. I think he died from natural causes within twelve years of the end of the war.

A.S. Williams was not wounded. He died a Congressman in Washington D.C. thirteen years after the war, on December 21, 1878, at age sixty-eight. A Brigadier General for the whole war, he remains obscure because he fought in so many lost Eastern Theater battles. But the reason for his silence about the orders packet has finally been resolved.

While the Confederacy launched no internal investigation, *Special Order 191's* loss forced Southern Arms to fight out of alignment from behind Antietam Creek on September 17. It remains the bloodiest day in American History, and directly affected the timing of the Emancipation Proclamation. These then are the amazing circumstances leading to America's elimination of slavery. But was not necessary to have remote viewed this target for historians to have realized that the finding of the Lost Order became history's foremost example of a spectacularly successful orphan.

* * *

Incredible opportunities with menacing consequences. At approximately 11:30 a.m., Adjutant Seth Williams handed General McClellan the packet. Upon looking at the orders, McClellan exclaimed out loud in public, "*Now I know what to do.*"[lx] He then broke off a meeting he was having with some local people about Federal troops in Frederick, Maryland and retired into his field tent. But one of those people was a Southern spy who went directly to Confederate Cavalry General JEB Stuart that evening, and relayed the story of McClellan's abrupt reaction to the Adjutant's transfer.

Evidential Details

Union General McClellan was now in procession of his enemy's orders as if he too was one of Robert E. Lee's Generals. He now knew Lee's army had been separated for over 72 hours; that Martinsburg and Harpers Ferry were targets; of the South's regrouping locations; and each enemy General's marching route.

But even with this, as was his character, McClellan developed reservations. He hesitated until 3 p.m. when he asked his cavalry commander to see if the lost dispatch *"order of march"* had been followed. Finally, at 6:20 p.m., he signed orders for Generals Franklin and Couch to move in the morning. Thus the precious hours of noon, to after 6 a.m. the next morning, had been squandered by the North - but not by the South.

In retrospect, few commanders in history have ever been given an equivalent opportunity to destroy an enemy as had been given George McClellan. With a quick and massive response, anyone, with 2-to-1 odds, would be able to defeat an opponent with his forces split five ways. The rebellion, east of the Appalachian Mountains, should now be over by the end of September. "The lost order represented the opportunity of a lifetime."[lxi] Robert E. Lee, and his Army of Northern Virginia, should now face the consequences.

At this point speculation is rife about delays. If marching orders had been issued to move to the mountains at 12:20, rather than 6:20 p.m., the next day's attack could have commenced at dawn, rather than the next afternoon. But McClellan also waited to order more force forward.

McMoneagle - My sense is that while deceit was never intentional by the loss of the object, there was a presumption of deceit that was felt by the Union commander, or decision maker; Sort of a sense that the Confederacy might be setting the Union up. In other words, that there might be a plan initiated to fool someone within the Union camp.

But, while the orders and map were absolutely accurate, they were not believed to be. My sense is that the Union Commander thought it was probably an act of disinformation. There was cause for some to suggest that they might be faked or a ruse to try and get the Union command to make the wrong decisions. So, they were never fully believed.

Though delayed, once it got under way, the Union advance did take Lee off guard. And his timetable had fallen behind schedule. "Not one of Lee's Harpers Ferry columns had conquered 191's stringent schedule. Not one (General) had attained its objective by Friday, September 12. Yet all were approaching their designated targets. Did one day really matter?"[lxii] McClellan's 18 hour overnight delay proved to be a critical factor in what would become a razor's edge struggle.

The Lost Orders made McClellan one of the most informed commanders in world history, but he could not see it. In *Landscape Turned Red,* author Stephen Sears wrote about how McClellan, "...managed to throw away the glittering opportunities for total victory offered him by the Lost Order..."[lxiii]

McMoneagle - General McClellan - Not much of a commander actually. I think he erred on the side of being too cautious. My sense is that this general was in fact too cautious all the way around. He I view as a weak and otherwise useless individual. He was, what I would call a Desk General, preferring to sit behind a desk in Washington, rather than lead men in the field. He didn't have the 'close with the enemy & kill the enemy' fervor that is required in a combat leader. I believe he will take the blame for many of the mistakes about to take place during the battles over the next three days.

In *George B. McClellan - The Young Napoleon,* Stephen Sears dedicates a chapter to the order. "September 13 was also the day the Federals' dismal intelligence gathering record took a startling upward turn with the discovery of the famous Lost Order." Sears continues, "The Lost Order represented the opportunity of a lifetime."[lxiv] Much has been made of McClellan's "extreme caution" after receiving Lee's orders. This was based on his certainty the Confederate Army was almost three times larger than it really was. But doubts about his state of mind have always run deeper.

As concerns McClellan's mentality, "Repeatedly he saw divine purpose in his being called to Washington to save the country. At the same time, he continually saw himself a victim of harassment. The personality revealed in all this is a mixture of complexes --- persecution, messianic, Napoleonic."[lxv] As a result, even with the Confederate battle plans, "...McClellan, by force of his temperament, succeeded in transforming himself into a badly misinformed commander."[lxvi] "...our impression that McClellan was eccentric, quite able to believe the unbelievable, is confirmed. We can give up trying to understand him."[lxvii]

McMoneagle – Could this man also have been manic depressive?

Joseph McMoneagle is the first and only remote viewer to be inducted into the American Psychological Association. He has lectured the Psychology Faculty at Harvard University. Here his decorated remote viewing capability provides history's first genuinely plausible psychiatric evaluation – on a dead man.

* * *

Evidential Details

Facing an unforeseen Union advance, a puzzled Robert E. Lee was forced to issue revised orders. He absolutely had to hold the line at the passes at South Mountain, while Jackson continued on to Harpers Ferry. He sent orders to General Daniel Harvey Hill.

D.H. Hill – "I received a note about midnight of the 13th from General Lee saying that he was not satisfied with the condition of things on the turnpike or National road, and directed me to go in person to Turner's Gap the next morning and assist (General) Stuart in its defense."[lxviii]

As he approached Hagerstown, Maryland Lee also ordered an increasingly disgruntled General Longstreet to countermarch his two divisions back 13 miles to support Hill's men at South Mountain. Riding over to Turner's Gap early on the 14th, Harvey Hill discovered a serious situation. From his position on the mountain, he looked out at the eastern horizon.

D.H. Hill – "...I had seen from the lookout station near the Mountain House the vast army of McClellan spread out before me. The marching columns extended back as far as the eye could see in the distance; it was a grand and glorious spectacle, and it was impossible to look at it without admiration. I had never seen so tremendous an army before, and did not see one like it afterward. ...here four corps were in full view, one of which was on the mountain and almost within rifle range."

As the battle progressed, it was a sight for Union soldiers as well. As he approached up the National Road to the pass in the Catoctin Mountains and looked across the valley at Confederate positions on South Mountain, a Union private recalled:

Miles Clayton Huyette: *"When we reached the summit where we could look down and across Middletown Valley - through the shimmering heat waves we could see lines of infantry - which looked like ribbons of blue - being rushed to the front; the rays of the sun glinted from musket... bayonet and polished brass cannon; batteries in position - in the fields in the valley - firing over the heads of the advancing line of battle; smoke of shells bursting in air at Crampton and Turner's Gaps, and could see lines of smoke in the woods near the summit of South Mountain - where the infantry boys were fighting in the brush among the rocks. It was a panoramic moving picture."*[lxix]

Hill knew his small force would have to fight alone until he was reinforced. He also knew that what was at stake was the imminent collapse of the Confederate eastern theater war effort.

D.H. Hill – "The sight inspired more satisfaction than discomfort; for though I knew my little force could be brushed aside as readily as the strong man can brush to one side the wasp or the hornet ...I hoped to be able to delay him (McClellan) until General Longstreet could come up and our (supply) trains could be extricated from their perilous position."[lxx]

Evidential Details

The Union advances at the Battle of South Mountain.

Evidential Details

"My division was very small and was embarrassed with the wagon trains and artillery of the whole army, save such as (Stonewall) Jackson had taken with him." "Had he (McClellan) made the movement which (Calvary Commander) Stuart and myself thought he was making, it was hardly possible for the little force under Lee ...to have escaped, encumbered as it was with wagon trains and reserve artillery. Forming his infantry into a solid column of attack, Lee might have cut a way through the fivefold force of his antagonist, but all the trains must have been lost, -- an irreparable loss to the South."[lxxi]

If the Union army forced its way through any of the gaps, Lee's army could be cut in two, defeated in detail, and his supply trains and cannon captured. But when D.H. Hill got over to Turner's Gap Calvary Commander JEB Stuart was gone. Only a 2/5 strength 200 man "regiment" under Thomas Rosser, with an artillery battery, remained. He also found General Alfred Colquitt's men had moved down the mountain and could not participate.

D.H. Hill – "In fact, after the removal of Colquitt's brigade, about 7 A.M., there was not a Southern soldier at the foot of the mountain until 3:30 P.M., when Captain (Robert E.) Park of the 12th Alabama Regiment was sent there with forty men."

Facing up to a bad situation, Hill opened with cannon when the Union forces came within range. Encountering resistance, Federal troops swung a mile south to Foxes Gap in an attempt to flank the Confederates. Here circumstances became extreme.

D.H. Hill – "Fifty skirmishers of the 5th North Carolina soon encountered the 23rd Ohio, deployed as skirmishers under Lieutenant-Colonel R. B. Hayes, afterward President of the United States. ...the action began at 9 am between (Union Major General Jacob) Cox's division and (Brigadier General Samuel) Garland's brigade."[lxxii]

General Cox had a 2 to 1 advantage over General Garland. Worse for Southern arms, Garland was mortally wounded in the midst of the battle on the mountain top. With their command structure in disarray, the Confederate units were mauled by the Federal onslaught.

D.H. Hill – "Garland's brigade, demoralized by his death and by the furious assault on its center, now broke in confusion and retreated behind the mountain, leaving some two hundred prisoners... The brigade was too roughly handled to be of any further use that day. There was nothing to oppose him (Cox). My other three brigades had not come up; I do not remember ever to have experienced a feeling of greater loneliness."[lxxiii]

Fox's Gap was now wide open for the Federal's to secure the high ground, come through and open the way for the whole Union army. From this point, they could cut off a southbound retreat for a third of the Confederate Army. The game appeared over. But in an incredible turn of events:

The Union Army (right edge) fought uphill against smaller Confederate forces.

<u>D.H. Hill</u> – "General Cox (Kanawha Division) seems not to have suspected that the defeat of Garland had cleared his front of every foe." "It was more than half an hour after the utter rout and dispersion of Garland's brigade when (Brigadier General) G. B. Anderson arrived at the head of his small but fine body of men." "Under the illusion that there was a large Confederate force on the mountain, the Federals withdrew to their first position in the morning to await the arrival of the other three divisions of (Union Major General Jessie) Reno's corps."[lxxiv]

"It was incomprehensible to us of the losing side that the (Union) men who charged us so boldly and repulsed our attacks so successfully should let slip the fruits of victory and fall back as though defeated." "Thus it was that a thin line of men extending for miles along the crest of the mountain could afford protection for so many hours to Lee's trains and artillery and could delay the Federal advance until (Lieutenant General) Longstreet's command did come up, and, joining with mine, saved the two wings of our forces. McClellan could have captured Lee's trains and artillery and interposed between Jackson and Longstreet before noon on that 14th of September."[lxxv]

In an incredible turn of fortune, Union forces did not move again until 4 p.m. But by 3:30 Longstreet's countermarching troops began relieving the Confederates at Turner's Gap. Meanwhile, over in Harpers Ferry, Stonewall Jackson's men began to set up their attack. His men worked around the clock, methodically positioning cannon to reduce the Federal stronghold.

So far, Southern arms had been fortunate. But once the Union Ninth Corp had all its men up an all-out attack was launched at Turner's Gap. A general battle raged up the middle, and on both sides, until sundown. Though the Confederates held their ground, they were severely outnumbered and could not continue. Lee then ordered Hill to withdraw by the morning of the 15$^{th.}$ But another critical day had been purchased.

Author 2000
General D.H. Hill's South Mountain battle Headquarters.

Six miles south, lay the pass at Crampton's Gap. A victory here would put Federal forces just five miles from Confederate General McLaws back at Harpers Ferry. Moving into position were the 19,500 men of the Union VI Corps under Major General William Buel Franklin [1823-1903]. His orders were to, *"cutoff, destroy or capture McLaws command and relieve* (Union) *Colonel Miles."*[lxxvi] There were only 1000 Southerners in this fight.

At noon, the forward division under Union Major General Henry Slocum encountered two regiments under Confederate Colonel William Parnham along with Thomas Munford's dismounted Calvary. Slocum's commanding officer described what happened.

General Franklin – "The enemy was driven in the utmost confusion from a position of strength and allowed no opportunity for even an attempt to rally, until the pass was cleared and in the possession of our troops." "The victory was complete, and its achievement followed so rapidly upon the first attack that the enemy reserves, although pushed forward on the double-quick, arrived but in time to participate in the flight, and add confusion to the rout."[lxxvii]

At 19 to 1 odds, the Rebels were devastated. And, at Harpers Ferry, Stonewall Jackson still had not opened his attack. How long that battle would

Evidential Details

last no one knew. The only certainty was that Crampton's Gap had been breached and General McLaws division at Harpers Ferry appeared subject to an overwhelming attack from behind.

Robert E. Lee sensed it was over. The mountain gaps had been breached and the Harpers Ferry assault was two days behind schedule. General Hill had withdrawn from South Mountain. Lee's army was split and demoralized at critical points. Prognosis for the next day - military disaster. So at 8 p.m. on the 14th, revised orders were issued to General McLaws.

R.E. Lee – "General: The day has gone against us and this army will go by Sharpsburg (Maryland) and cross the (Potomac) river. It is necessary for you to abandon your position tonight."

But four hours earlier Stonewall's men had phased in an artillery barrage against the Union garrison at Harpers Ferry. While time consuming, southern artillery had been well positioned in the hills. Then the rebel signal corp. coordinated point blank cannon fire from the surrounding hilltops that raged until sundown.

"The great circle of artillery (fired) to a common center, while the clouds of smoke, rolled up from the tops of the various mountains, and the thunder of the guns reverberating among them, gave the idea of so many volcanoes."[lxxviii] The Union position was now virtually indefensible. One soldier wrote, "*The infernal screech owls (Confederate shells) came hissing and singing, then bursting, plowing great holes in the earth, filling our eyes with dust, and tearing many giant trees to atoms.*"[lxxix] Union counter fire was ineffective in its efforts to shoot uphill at the Confederates.

During the night, Jackson moved his cannon forward while, at 8 p.m., Union Colonel Benjamin Davis led his 1500 man Calvary across a Potomac River pontoon bridge and rode 50 miles in 12 hours to escape Confederate forces in the area. As the Army of Northern Virginia congealed behind Antietam Creek, D.H. Hill, remarked:

D.H. Hill - "But from whatever standpoint it may be looked at, the Battle of South Mountain must be of interest to the military reader as showing the effect of a hallucination in enabling 9000 men to hold 30,000 at bay for so many hours..."[lxxx]

At dawn, Southern cannon opened at Harper's Ferry with a vengeance and by approximately 7:30 a.m., the Federals ran out of artillery shells. The surrender ceremony was complete by eight o'clock. General Jackson collected the 12-13,000 captured small arms, 200 hundred wagons, 1200 mules and 73 cannon, while A. P. Hill's division hurried to support Lee at Sharpsburg, Maryland.

After the war, Lee claimed he was out to crush McClellan. Regarding the stakes, General Walker said Lee told him directly:

Evidential Details

The Potomac River in 1862 and the "common center" at Harpers Ferry. The Shenandoah River enters just past the house (middle right edge). The Federal's in town were pounded by Generals Walker and McLaws left and right from the heights across the rivers. Here the Historian can visualize the close to point blank range enjoyed by Southern cannoneers. This camera angle does not show the Federal defense perimeter against Stonewall Jackson's Bolivar Heights land assault which originated from the cameraman's right.

Evidential Details

<u>R.E. Lee</u>: "'I shall concentrate the army at Hagerstown (Maryland)...and march to this point,' placing his finger at Harrisburg, Pennsylvania. 'That is the objective point of the campaign.'"[lxxxi]

The target was the railroad bridge over the Susquehanna River which, if destroyed, would shut down the North's ability to move material by rail in an east - west direction. Lee would attempt the same objective again in July, 1863. His efforts culminated in a decisive three day affair in a sleepy little Pennsylvania hamlet called Gettysburg. But in 1862, "...the final unforeseen factor affecting Lee's strategy was the finding of the famous document known to history as the 'Lost Dispatch'."[lxxxii]

With Northern newspaper stories and testimony before a Conduct of the War Joint Congressional Committee in March 1863, Lost Order speculation abounded.[14] Both sides wanted answers to the intriguing question about how the packet had been lost, and who lost it. So, as this target was submitted to McMoneagle's office in 1997, Civil War historians agreed that, "In the absence of new evidence, it seems unlikely that there will ever be a solution to the mystery of how Order 191 was lost."[lxxxiii]

* * *

Who, how, why, exactly when and even where the orders were lost, has been the Civil War's most significant mystery ever since. Some historians have even written about the possibility of ending the war thirty-one months early. "Lee called the enemy's possession of the order, '*a great calamity*'"[lxxxiv]

Some implicate General Hill simply because he was the addressee. But could we confirm that the man, who for the rest of his life hotly denied losing the orders, was really to blame? Daniel Harvey Hill assures us: "*It is the unusual that impresses.*"[lxxxv]

A glimpse of D.H. Hill's life shows that in many ways he was his own worst enemy. He graduated from West Point 28th in a class of 56 in 1842. But he was an instigator. For example, he thought it was a good idea to bypass the Army's chain of command by going directly to Confederate President Jefferson Davis with a lack of vigilance report on the part of the Cavalry. He then openly questioned the Cavalry's manhood with his standing "joke" of a $50.00 cash reward for anyone finding a dead solider with spurs on. Later, due to Hill's ongoing criticisms, he had to be prevented

---

[14] The *New York Herald* and the *Washington Star* newspapers published partially correct stories about the lost order on September 15, 1862. The origin of the Congressional leaks has never been determined, but a press connected George A. Custer had access to this information through a Cavalry staff meeting.

Evidential Details

from fighting a duel with non-West Point Brigadier General Robert Toombs over troop handling issues. In writings to his wife, Isabella Morrison Hill, he referred to Confederate Congressmen as "fools."

The problem was that Harvey Hill knew right from wrong. The youngest of 13 children, he had an intelligently "grim demeanor" with an educatedly derisive wit that he used to expose shortcomings in others. In a military school instructional manner, he liked to point out how a stranger could better himself.

Hill also had impeccable religious credentials as one who could forthrightly instruct another how best to turn their life away from sin. And he was clear on his duty to proffer freelance spiritual guidance to help men save their souls. General Longstreet said, "*He was a bitter, sarcastic critic of the frailties of humans.*"[lxxxvi]

It was said Hill could even be "*eccentric on the verge of wrong-headedness.*"[lxxxvii] In a paraphrased statement from the ever reserved Robert E. Lee it was recounted that he thought, "*D.H. Hill had such a queer temperament he could never tell what to expect from him.*"[lxxxviii]

It was also because of being a West Point graduate that being under suspicion of losing the order, and then being suspected of lying about it, led to a hapless military career. Because Hill was a fighter, he had hung on at the South Mountain battle. Then he went on with General Gordon to fight in the horrific Confederate center at the battle of Antietam known as the sunken road, or "Bloody Lane". But the way he expressed himself was not what military men wanted to hear.

D.H. Hill: "The battle of South Mountain was one of extraordinary illusions and delusions."[lxxxix]

It is unclear when Harvey Hill first realized McClellan had been in possession of the lost order. In correspondence Hill wrote, "That an order from Lee directed to me was lost, I do not now doubt."[xc] But he would continue to deny having received it. He even had his adjutant Major Rachford[15] sign an affidavit stating he had not received it. Daniel Harvey Hill vociferously protested his innocence, and it was not in his character to be wrong or lose face. Still dogged by inquiries over 15 years later, in 1880 he wrote:

D.H. Hill: "This order...was addressed to me, but I proved twenty years ago that it could not have been lost through my neglect or carelessness."

What the proof was that you had not done something was unclear.

---

[15] Major Rachford (1840-1910) was Hill's mathematics student at Davidson College in 1858, and was dedicated to the General which is why he was his staff officer. He wrote his memoir but no determination on who lost *Special Order 191* was made.

Evidential Details

Hill also floated the idea of treachery. But going forward post war credibility would be important as he interviewed for the University of Arkansas Presidency [1877-1884], and then in 1885, President of today's Georgia Military College in Milledgeville, GA.

Near life's end, he was afflicted with painful stomach cancer. General Daniel Harvey Hill, 68, died in September of 1889 - twenty-seven years to the month that the lost orders were found. On his deathbed his last words were, *"Almost there."*

* * *

Owing to Hill's staunch denials about losing the orders, and a lack of proof, there have been many theories as to who lost the dispatch. Ever since, many have looked elsewhere and substantial research has been conducted on every other connected individual. One plausible explanation has been that Jackson's courier, Henry Kyd Douglas, dropped the orders. So now it was time for McMoneagle to solve this mystery.

McMoneagle - Dress profile - I see a man dressed in Confederate Gray with gold braid sewn into the sleeves and edges... He is wearing a single large gold star on his collar. Man who loses [the] packet has three stars on his collar, single line of braid across both cuffs.

Regardless of rank, a Confederate General's collar eliminates couriers, staff and support personnel. What is confusing is that Confederate General's regalia contained one large star in the middle of three, but this did not mean the soldier was a Lieutenant General. Harvey Hill had been a Major General since March 27, 1862. So this single component was inconclusive.

McMoneagle - Shorter than most; about five feet, six inches in height. Sandy colored hair about 145 pounds, green piercing eyes... Whether the man had pale blue or pale green eyes, my color maybe a little off, but that man had pale eyes. He has a heavy...beard but no mustache. He is riding a "roan" [dark red-brown horse which almost looks black]. He limps.

In *Joseph E. Johnston - A Civil War Biography* author Craig L. Symonds indicates, "Hill was small and fine-boned, with lank blond hair and pale blue eyes."[xci] Available photographs also showed Hill's eyes were so pale they can be observed with archaic 1860's camera equipment. This cannot be said about the other Confederate Generals in the Maryland campaign.

But was there any information about a Southern General with slightness of build, the lack of a mustache and limping? These were

Evidential Details

historically unheard of evidential details. While no photographic evidence exists, research did find references to these descriptions for one Officer.

About D.H. Hill, C.D. Fishburne remarked: *"He was then comparatively a young man, wore full whiskers but no mustache, was slightly built, of serious aspect..."*[xcii] So, Hill was known to have differentiated himself from the normal bearded look by shaving his mustache. None of the other Maryland campaign Generals were known to make this shaving effort.

Regarding intermittent stiffness forcing a limp, research turned up: *"A slender, well-proportioned man not long past 40, of medium height and erect military posture, except when pain from a chronic spinal ailment forced him to bend slightly..."*[xciii]

Bending slightly as he walked would have accounted for the appearance of limping. None of the other Confederate Generals limped. So, what about his personality? The Wilmington Messenger newspaper wrote about Hill: *"He was what he seemed. There was no hypocrisy or guile or sham about him."*[xciv]

McMoneagle – He is stern, doesn't drink, his only vice being probably smoking a pipe or cigars. He has a reputation of being very "uncompromising" and historically doesn't listen to his men or seek advice. My sense is that he is a deeply religious man... A no nonsense kind of person who is both liked and disliked for his black and white views. No gray areas within this person's thinking; probably aggressive and unforgiving in a sense. The guy who was in charge of the (Confederate) **camp is the man who rides the Roan horse.**

Of the five Generals reporting to Lee that fall, this psychological profile is best fitted to Daniel Harvey Hill and Stonewall Jackson. But Hill presents the best combination of physical characteristics. And so now we learn how the Special order was lost.

McMoneagle - The man who lost the packet was mounting his horse to join his men who were encamped nearby. Everyone was packing up camp and moving. They were just given orders on where they were moving to and why. The packet was dropped when he was alone but he was in the process of joining up with others. I get a sense that he went to his horse, which was back away from where the tents were being taken down. His was the last horse there.

This object or package probably belongs to a very important individual within the Confederacy; someone who has himself known that he has lost this. He honestly lost the object in question, which was probably some kind of a dispatch or letter. When he mounted his horse, the packet was lost. Packet was lost as the man carrying it was climbing into his saddle. I see him putting it into an inside coat pocket,

Evidential Details

but missing the pocket all together, having it quickly slide out from inside his jacket while either mounting or riding his horse. He didn't notice the loss of the packet. Once he was in the saddle, he joined others who were marching away from or out of the camp area. The packet laid on the ground more than 24 hours...

McMoneagle RV Art - Evidential Details ©1997

General D.H. Hill's 1862 Campground Close-up
This sketch shows Confederate troop areas, tents, gun emplacements and where the orders were dropped. On the lower right, it says: **Lost pouch left here.**

Hill was viewed limping, signaling discomfort from his spinal ailment when he was handling the packet. Nagging (slipped disc?) pain made it easier to fail to notice the orders were dropped. It would also make it easier to miss his jacket's inside pocket.

This can be understood by observing a man mounting a horse with back pain severe enough to make him limp. Imagine, with his left hand holding the saddle post, Hill was in motion to swing his right leg, shoulder

Evidential Details

blade, and arm over the horse while attempting to insert a packet into his left coat pocket. If the orders packet did not seat into the pocket properly, it would have slipped down inside as the coat was closed. Most business men, even without a spinal ailment, will undershoot their inside suit coat pocket sooner or later. This is particularly true if they attempt to insert a packet without holding the jacket with their other hand.

McMoneagle – I believe he later thought that he had left it in a tent back at the camp he had left earlier in the day. He regretted losing the packet, but it was not a big deal for him, as he believed it to be safe with someone else (Lt Colonel Andersen) **at the camp. He knew his orders for the day and the following week, so he would not have needed the packet to get his job done.**

The information in the packet was a copy of the same information given to at least a handful of men (Generals). **Each packet of information contained the specifics for an overall plan of action that would be associated with the coming battle. Ultimately, the packet was not essential to the man who lost it. I have a sense that he was one of the three or four other officers who were given like copies or near similar copies of the same thing.**

It was left lying on the ground under a tree approximately twenty-five yards from where the General's and other officer's tents were pitched. The tents were struck and the camp moved within two hours of the loss of the packet.

The packet was dropped away from the Officer's tents in the Officer's horse grouping area. Previously, where the orders were dropped, in fact where Hill's campground was located, has been in dispute. After the war, Daniel Harvey Hill strenuously denied anyone having authority to sign for the orders ever received it. Hill received his instructions from Stonewall Jackson's command and was not in need of a copy from Lee's Headquarters. True, but telling the Theater Commander you do not need his orders was strange. Receiving orders directly from the top represented upward mobility in the command structure which Hill certainly would have wanted.

Politically imaging is important to any General with a new direct report. What Robert E. Lee thought mattered and something was not right here. Whether a staff orderly had signed for the orders was not Lee's bottom line. Top secret order of battle plans had been mishandled putting the entire Southern war effort in jeopardy. It would make sense that whoever lost the orders had a second copy. How else could he operate over a week without an inquiry to headquarters about not receiving orders? So, how did the packet arrive?

McMoneagle – It was read to him by his Chief of Staff, a colonel,

Evidential Details

who got it from a courier [rider] (Henry Kyd Douglas).

Civil War Library and Museum

Confederate Major General Daniel Harvey Hill
Shown with a moustache, the historian can confirm his eyes
light shading and how the three stars on his collar were situated.

So the orders were read to Hill by his Assistant Adjutant Colonel 23 year old Archer Anderson. This confirms Hill's adjutant Rachford had not lied when he signed the affidavit stating he never received the orders. It is just that Hill had the wrong man swear. We could find no documentation that either Officer mentioned this event again. But it was clear the order had been mishandled in Harvey Hill's camp.[16]

The insider probabilities were that courier Douglas swore he delivered the orders to Hill's camp, and General Jackson acknowledged he had sent Hill a second copy. Faced with this technically unsubstantiated innuendo, Hill wrote his old adversary George McClellan a letter dated April 17, 1869. In it, he stated that all Confederate orders packets were returned to headquarters after the orders were removed. The fact the orders packet was found intact proved Hill was innocent.

But old adversary McClellan was not in a position to verify Confederate Staff Officer operational details. It does however show the length Hill was prepared to go to win support for a cause that no longer mattered excepting pride and vindication. But, if there is a "smoking gun" of doubt, it would be to understand Hill's need to proclaim that the orders loss actually saved the day!

D.H. Hill: "In the battle of South Mountain the imaginary forces of the Lost Dispatch were worth more to us than ten thousand men."[xcv] "The ten imaginary regiments of the Lost Dispatch retarded his (General John Gibbon's) progress through the woods..." "There were only a few skirmishers on his right, but the lost dispatch made him believe otherwise." "The loosing of the dispatch was the saving of Lee's army."[xcvi]

Hill wrote this even though the lost orders did not mention regiments and that Gibbon (1827-1896) did not have a copy. Curiously, D.H. Hill would be the only Confederate to make positive statements about the packet's loss. But why try to sanctify the South's worst security breach that resulted in having to scramble to avoid disaster? And then to go into a congratulatory mode about it being the Army of Northern Virginia's saving grace was simply beyond belief.

This aggravated Robert E. Lee who was then Washington College President. In uncharacteristic manner, on February 15, 1868, he indignantly condemned Hill's remarks to a college clerk named E.C. Gordon who jotted his comments down. Later that day Lee complained to Professor William Allan, who went on to become an Army of Northern Virginia historian. Still grousing a week later, Lee wrote D.H. Hill about the lost orders on February 21, saying:

---

[16] Archer Anderson (1838-1918) was the son of Confederate General Joseph R. Anderson who owned the fabled Tredegar Iron Works in Richmond, Virginia. Severely wounded at Antietam Creek, he went on to fight in the Army of Tennessee and gave speeches about the Battle of Chickamauga after the war. In 1892 he became Tredegar's President.

Evidential Details

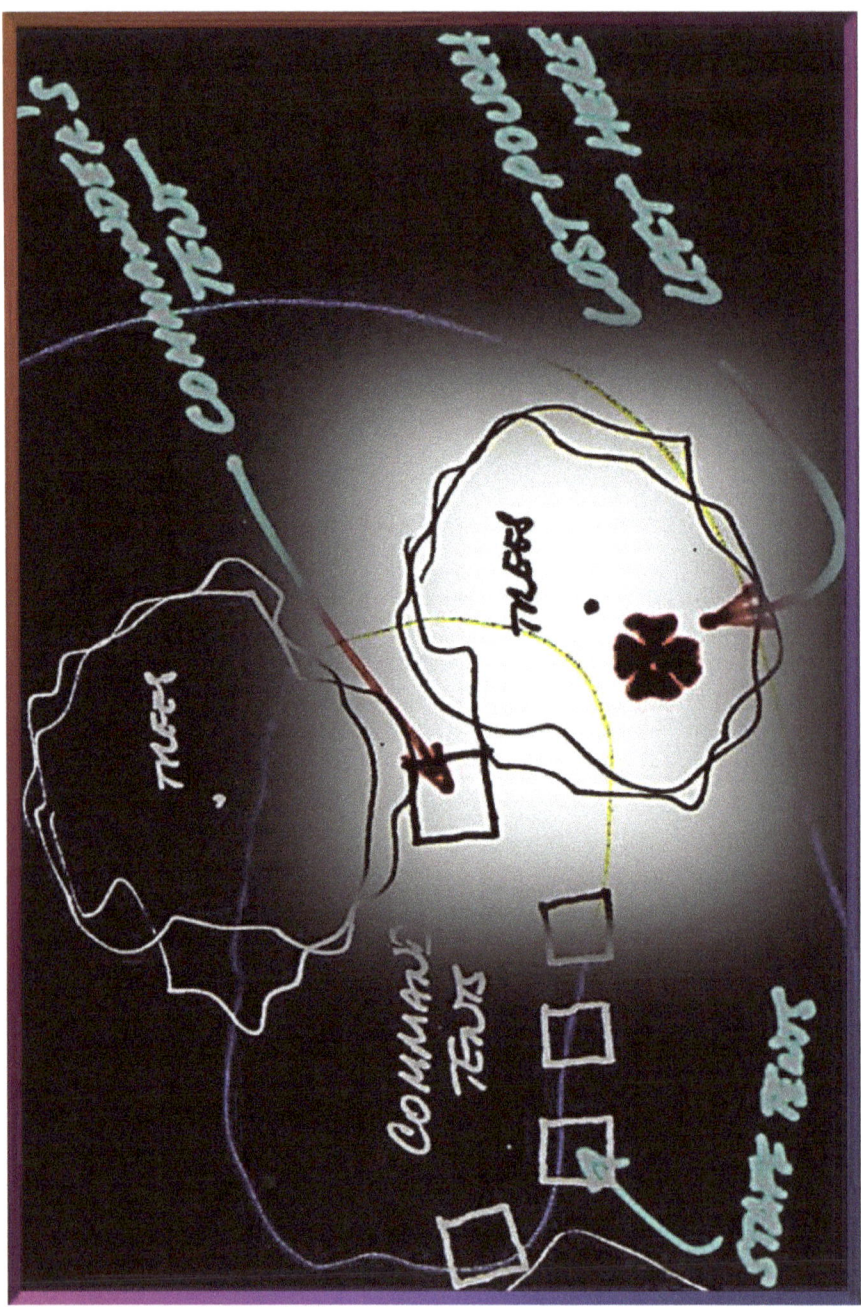

McMoneagle RV Art – Evidential Details ©1997

Confederate Command Tent Close-up

In the military, McMoneagle was tasked with how and where various clandestine transactions took place. In this case he details the distance between the Command tents and where the packet was dropped.

Evidential Details

"I consider it a great calamity...", and that, *"...subsequent reflection has not caused me to change my opinion."*[xcvii]

McClellan's delayed troop movements allowed Harpers Ferry to be captured. It also allowed the South to regroup behind Antietam Creek enabling Lee's 45,000 men (38,000 effectives) to fight the 87,000 Federal's[xcviii] to a tactical draw. What should have been an easy Union victory with these odds became a Southern victory of sorts.

As the sun rose the next morning, the Army of Northern Virginia, now about 28,500 strong, started moving their wounded south to the Potomac River, while waiting for an attack from McClellan's remaining 74,500 men. None came. As the Confederate army slipped away, 32,000 Union soldiers had not participated in what turned into a strategic victory for the North as the Union Army occupied the field.

McMoneagle – Southern retreat - I think the (Potomac) **river crossing is important as I get a sense that the Southern Army was allowed to retreat across it, when all the Union had to do was pin them with their backs to the river and the war might have ended long before it even really got started. Such a move most certainly would have eradicated nearly an entire army of the South.**

For his failure to press the enemy, George McClellan was again relieved of command. In the 1864 elections, he was the Democratic Presidential candidate who ran against Abraham Lincoln. In that campaign, the Democratic Party Platform called for an immediate cease fire while sizable Confederate armies remained in the field.

So in September of 1862, Confederate arms were checked in the State of Maryland northwest of Washington. Lee had lost control of events and was unable to fight at his chosen place with his forces aligned as he would have preferred. The finding of the lost order made the difference in battle location, the campaign's outcome, and hence, the Emancipation Proclamation's timing.

Overall, the Maryland Campaign resulted in 27,475 Union losses including those captured at Harpers Ferry and the Battles at South Mountain. Confederate losses were reported at 12,392. Assuming 66 more men on each side died or were taken captive, a 40,000 man rounded combined total of dead, missing, wounded or captured, from September 12 to 17 is reasonable. The removal of 40,000 men, between the ages of 16 and 36, would comprise approximately 22.5% of a large city of the day with 175,000 inhabitants. In just five days, every male in this age bracket would disappear. Such was the carnage in America's Civil War.

How *Special Order 191* was lost has always been the most

important mystery in the Civil War. And its significance was even more pronounced when London and Paris decided not to extend diplomatic recognition to Richmond's commercial attaché offices. While sympathetic to the South for their desire for quality cotton and tobacco, they finalized their decision based on the outcome at Antietam Creek.

As the Illinois Republican Senatorial candidate in 1858, Lincoln had established his pro-emancipation credentials well. So much so that, his 1860 Presidential victory was a signal to the South to take up secession. But Lincoln waited to issue the proclamation until he had some success on the battlefield. After Antietam, Abraham Lincoln [1809-1865] came forward and told his Secretaries in a cabinet meeting that, *"God had decided this question in favor of the slaves."*[xcix] Within eighteen months, he had transformed the war into a dual cause to abolish slavery as well as preserve the Union.

This nation saw the result of the Lost Order when, on November 4, 2008, one legacy of this mystery was realized. It was on that day Barak Hussein Obama was elected President of the United States. Because of the Lost Order, "The course of the war and the course of the nation were forever changed as a result."[c]

Aftermath

The direct military results of the lost order were the Battles of South Mountain and Antietam Creek. The day after the battle at Antietam Creek, Lee held his ground while the army evacuated its trains of wounded across the Potomac at Shepherdstown, Virginia.

The 12,419 Union prisoners captured at Harpers Ferry were not sent south. Instead, they were paroled by raising their right hands and swearing an oath in unison not to serve against the Confederacy until such time as an equal number of Southern men were paroled. Each officer had to sign a statement.

The Union parolees started a two day march to Frederick, M.D. on the 16th, and went on to Annapolis, Maryland. The Army decided not to furlough the men instead railing them to Chicago's Camp Douglas on September 23. Their final destination was Minnesota where they were to fight the Sioux Indians under General Pope's command. However, they were never sent because most of the officers were recalled to Washington to testify at the Harpers Ferry disaster Military Court of Inquiry.

On September 25, 1862, the Secretary of War (Defense) opened a commission, *"to investigate the circumstances of the abandonment of Maryland Heights"* which led directly to Harper's Ferry's surrender. Since commanding officer Dixon S. Miles had been killed with what seemed the last artillery shell blast, the ax fell on 32nd Ohio's Colonel Thomas H. Ford.

On November 8, he was, *"dismissed from the service of the United States"*, for having conducted his Maryland Heights defense, *"without ability, abandoned his position without sufficient cause, and has shown throughout such a lack of military capacity as to disqualify him, in the estimation of the Commission, for a command in the service."*[ci] All the Harpers Ferry prisoners were declared exchanged by January 10, 1863.

On October 3, President Lincoln traveled to the Antietam battlefield to confer with General McClellan. Questions arose as to why the retreating Confederates had not been pressed against the Potomac River. McClellan's commitment to the Union cause has subsequently come into question and this may have been in the back of the President's mind.

On July 7, 1862, just two months before the finding of the lost order, McClellan had handed President Lincoln a letter at Harrison's Landing in Virginia. The letter said in part that Federal: *"Military power should not be allowed to interfere with the relations of servitude, either by supporting or impairing the authority of the master..."*[cii] This mirrored the Confederate Congress's stance.

During that summer, President Lincoln had been working on his Emancipation Proclamation. On July 22, 1862, it was read to his cabinet. Now, due to the Lost Order, the President had the victory he needed to issue his proclamation. The new law read in part:

That on the 1st day of January A.D. 1863, all persons held as slaves within any State or designated part of a State...shall be then, thence-forward, and forever free...

And I further declare and make known that such persons of suitable condition will be received into the armed service of the United States to garrison forts, positions, stations, and other places, and to man vessels of all sorts in said service.

And upon this act, sincerely believed to be an act of justice, warranted by the Constitution...I invoke the considerate judgment of mankind and the gracious favor of Almighty God.

Addendum

Next page is Confederate General Thomas J. Jackson's rewritten orders to General Daniel Harvey Hill. Here the historian can review the top secret orders Union General McClellan had in his possession as the Confederate Army was split five ways.

Evidential Details

Special Orders, No. 191
HEADQUARTERS, ARMY OF NORTHERN VIRGINIA
September 9th, 1862

The Army will resume its march tomorrow, taking the Hagerstown road. General Jackson's command will form the advance, and after passing Middletown, with such portions as he may select, take the route toward Sharpsburg, cross the Potomac at the most convenient point, and by Friday night take possession of the Baltimore and Ohio Railroad, capture such of the enemy as may be at Martinsburg, and intercept such as may attempt to escape from Harpers Ferry.

General Longstreet's command will pursue the same road as far as Boonsboro', where it will halt with the reserve, supply, and baggage trains of the army.

General McLaws with his own division and that of General R.H. Anderson, will follow General Longstreet; on reaching Middle-town he will take the route to Harpers Ferry, and by Friday morning possess himself of the Maryland Heights and endeavor to capture the enemy at Harpers Ferry and vicinity.

General Walker, with his division after accomplishing the object in which he is now engaged, will cross the Potomac at Check's ford, ascend its right bank to Lovettsville, take possession of Loudoun Heights, if practicable, by Friday morning, Keyes's ford on his left, and the road between the end of the mountain and the Potomac on his right. He will, as far as practicable, cooperate with General McLaws and General Jackson in intercepting the retreat of the enemy.

General D.H. Hill's division will form the rearguard of the army, pursuing the road taken by the main body. The reserve artillery, ordnance, and supply trains, etc., will precede General Hill.

General Stuart will detach a squadron of cavalry to accompany the commands of Generals Longstreet, Jackson, and McLaws, and, with the main body of the cavalry, will cover the route of the army and bring up all stragglers that may have been left behind.

The commands of Generals Jackson, McLaws, and Walker, after accomplishing the objects for which they have been detached, will join the main body of the army at Boonsboro' or Hagerstown.

Each regiment of the march will habitually carry its axes in the regimental ordinance-wagons, for use of the men at their encampments, to procure wood, etc.

By command of General R.E. Lee.
R. H. Chilton, Assistant Adjutant-General.
Major-General D.H. Hill, Command Division.

Evidential Details

Copy of Special Order 191

Lead-sealed targeting envelops stored in private safes, ...analysis of dozens of independent scientific studies, hundreds of evaluations, an entire army of scientists and oversight committees focused on providing protection against fraud, and periodic reviews for over a twenty-five-year period cannot seem to persuade those who will always find a reason to doubt the existence of the paranormal.

~ Joseph McMoneagle - *The Ultimate Time Machine* ~

Book II

Evidential Details

The Last Moments of

General George Armstrong Custer

at the

Battle of the

Little Bighorn

with History's only
image of Indian Chief

Crazy Horse

Evidential Details

> Ye say they all have pass't away,
> That noble race and brave,
> That their light canoes have vanish'd
> From off the crested wave;
> That, 'mid the forests where they roam'd,
> There rings no hunter's shout;
> But their name is on your waters,
> Ye may not wash it out.
>
> *Lydia Huntley Sigourney*

Whether power ever pays homage has never been more at issue than in the struggle between the Native American Indian and the European for control of the North American Hemisphere. Our story opens in 1876 as the United States 44th Congress cut the nation's armed forces budget. Decisions had to be made.

Among the military issues was how to get Native American Indians – primarily Sioux and Cheyenne – to return peaceably to their designated homelands. These two tribes presented the greatest challenges to the reservation system and for many, represented an attractive rejectionist beacon. Moreover, they had disrupted the building of the transcontinental railroad. Those troubles had begun just after the Civil War in 1867 when Cheyenne Chief Turkey Foot wrecked a train at Plume Creek, some 230 miles west of Omaha, Nebraska. Surveyors were executed, track ripped up, telegraph lines cut and Chinese rail workers killed.

In spite of setbacks, and with some mountain "techno-marvels", the world's first trans-continental railway celebration took place on May 10, 1869. This was an expansion of the machine age and with it, the pace of change in the West changed. The world could now travel and trade directly across the continent in a week rather than taking 100 days to sail 14,300 miles around South America through the treacherous Straits of Magellan. Coast to coast, through the Rocky Mountains and the High Sierra, this was the completion of the world's largest industrial enterprise to date.

These rails welded a dream that introduced a tremendous diversity of cultures, cuisines and products promoting a continental size democracy. It would be this same grand industrial "can do" attitude that connected the oceans through Panama just 40 years later.

For over four centuries the beleaguered North American Indian had clashed with soldiers or mercenaries from most of the European powers. Even the Alaskan Aleut Eskimo population had been reduced from 30,000 to 3,000 when the Russians left in 1867.[ciii] Now, in the struggle's last 100

Evidential Details

years (1790–1890), Native Americans faced the United States Army with its post-Civil War enhanced technology, its veterans, and its vast weapons stockpile. The Government's Indian Affairs Bureau had been part of the Department of War (Defense), from 1824 to 1849 when it was transferred to the Department of the Interior. Now in his second term, the victorious Civil War General, President Ulysses S. Grant (1822-1885) had been in office since March 4, 1869.

As westward expansion continued, the public viewed the government's role as guardian of citizens and commerce. Washington's mind-set was that members, of what became today's 562 recognized Indian tribes, would farm or leave the reservation by offering a marketable skill.

As usual, the U.S. Department of State had Foreign Policy objecttives. But because of its raw materials base, heavy industry and professional expertise, the United States as adjacent to this or that Indian Nation had not worked well for Native Americans. As in Europe, the foreign affairs concern was that, "The interaction between national goals and the resources for attaining them is the perennial subject of statecraft."[civ]

But the Indians did not interpret the world in this manner. Their intertribal relations consisted of unresolvable ancient feuding coupled with what was many times a purely episodic personality cult response to external affairs. Other than the immediate "defend this territory" objective, there was no long range planning which is a result of a barter economy with no alphabet. Without a Pan-Indian consensus, "…it is nonetheless true that nations can, and not infrequently do, find their goals selected for them by outside events."[cv]

This meant that regarding the concept of international relations, even the most elemental basis for modern territorial recognition – postal exchange – was absent. The Plaines Indians also depended upon their enemy for weaponry and ammunition. Holding impeccable anti-immigration credentials, they were endlessly involved in expansionist crisis management. Native American councils discussed "Pale Face" migration and relied on a Calvary approach to hold ill-defined borders. As the nibbling process continued, the Tribes' hunting range diminished, and they were forced to go "on the warpath" to protect the territory required to support what was - in many cases - a hunter-gatherer life style.

<u>G.A. Custer</u>: *If I were an Indian, I often think that I would greatly prefer to cast my lot among those of my people who adhered to the free open plains rather than submit to the confined limits of a reservation.*[cvi]

Back east, the word was, *go west young man* as hopeful homesteaders set out across a thousand mile front seeking a better life like modern illegals. Then threatened settlers clamored for protection from the gruesome hacking deaths described by an Eastern press as outrages against humanity.

As we approach this battle, what remains untaught is that, "In the early stages of American industrialization (1850-1890), output per man-hour grew at an *annual* rate of 1.5 percent;"[cvii] So, in the Washington style geo-political arena, by 1876, the idea that Indian boundary disputes were subject to a European style declaration of war became absurd. Nor did the Indians send representatives east to monitor treaty terms. The result was that a virtually non-stop platoon level guerilla war broke out from the end of the Civil War to 1890.

During the Grant Administration, these hard scrabble realities congealed in a kind of "New Deal" mindset. A peaceful resolution, it was thought, could be found by offering all Native Americans U.S. citizenship. In his Second Annual address to Congress, on December 5, 1870, President Grant declared:

I entertain the confident hope that the policy now pursued will in a few years bring all the Indians upon reservations, where they will live in houses and have schoolhouses and churches, and will be pursuing peaceful and self-sustaining avocations... I call your special attention to the report of the Commissioner of Indian Affairs for full information on this subject...[cviii]

He was referring to the U.S. Government's Board of Indian Commissioners Report that read, in part:

...it must be admitted that the actual treatment they (Indians) *have received has been unjust and iniquitous beyond the power of words to express."* And that, *"measures attempted by the government for their advancement have been almost uniformly thwarted by the agencies employed to carry them out."* This was because, *"The agent, appointed to be their friend and counselor, business manager, and the almoner of the government bounties, frequently went among them only to enrich himself in the shortest possible time, at the cost of the Indians, and spend the largest available sum of the government money with the least ostensible beneficial result."*

<u>G.A. Custer</u>: *Cultivation, such as the white man would give him, deprives him of his identity. Education...seems to weaken rather than strengthen his intellect.*[cix]

Also remarkably untaught is that previous treaties emerged as an obstruction to citizenship. In order for the Indians to achieve a more secure future it was recommended, "The treaty system should be abandoned, and as soon as any just method can be devised to accomplish it, existing treaties

Evidential Details

should be abrogated."[cx] Seneca tribe Indian Commissioner Ely Parker elaborated:

The Indians...should be that of wards of the government; the duty of the latter being to protect them, to educate them in industry, the arts of civilization... (and to) elevate them to the rights of citizenship... Every means in the power of the government and its agents should be employed to render settlement and industrious habits on the reservation attractive and certain in its rewards. Furthermore, after being surveyed, "inalienable" land titles should be deeded and the civilized tribes now in Indian territory should be taxed, and made citizens of the United States as soon as possible.

<u>G. A. Custer</u>: *In making this change, the Indian has to sacrifice all that is dear to his heart. He abandons the only mode of life in which he can be a warrior and win triumphs and honors worthy to be sought after. And in taking up the pursuits of the white man, he does that which he has always been taught, from his earliest infancy, to regard as degrading to his manhood, to labor, to work for his daily bread, an avocation suitable only for squaws.*[cxi]

Nevertheless, the administration saw this approach as their best prospect to put an end to frontier bloodshed, and hence had a civil obligation to implement. The evidence indicated a majority of the tribes wanted a predictable system that provided a just, equitable and timely distribution of their treaty supplies.

Therefore, in what was hoped to be America's nineteenth century Common Era, Republican President Grant signed the Fifteenth Constitutional Amendment which protected voting rights for all specifying:

The right of citizens of the United States to vote shall not be denied or abridged by the United States or by any State on account of race, color, or previous condition of servitude.

For all this, President Grant enjoyed fellow Republican woman's rights leader Susan B. Anthony's (1847-1906) support. However, while the Indian homeland concept appealed to the Administration, there were powerful Indian Chiefs who scoffed at U.S. citizenship or of the reservation system.

<u>G. A. Custer</u>: (I like) *Looking at him as the fearless hunter, the matchless horseman and warrior of the plains...and contrasting him with the reservation Indian...who in reality is groveling in beggary, bereft of many of the qualities which in his wild state tended to render him noble...*[cxii]

* * *

Evidential Details

The transcontinental railroad's tremendous success led to plans to lay a northern route through the Dakotas and Montana connecting Minneapolis, Minnesota with Seattle, Washington. Taking advantage of vagueness in the Treaty of 1868 regarding what territory had been ceded between the Bighorn Mountains and the Yellowstone River, engineers moved to lay track west of Bismarck, The Dakota Territory. During the summers of the early 1870's, military escorts accompanied surveyors into the area. Looking for action, Civil War Cavalry Officer, General George Armstrong Custer, was scouting in advance of the army. He found what he was looking for and wound up fighting two sharp engagements during the summer of 1873.

Back east President Grant knew the military term for Indian warfare was "unconventional" and that this garnered little respect in Congressional appropriations hearings. But as Supreme Commander Grant also knew, just as was re-learned 100 years later in Vietnam, many times the American Indian was, "...an enemy who usually could not be clearly identified and differentiated from kinsman not disposed at the moment to be enemies. Indians could change with bewildering rapidity from friend to foe to neutral, and rarely could one be confidently distinguished from another."[cxiii]

As in Vietnam, soldiers angered by the denial of a clear-cut result became frustrated. And this denial was on Custer's mind as he peered through his field glasses that afternoon.

On December 6, 1875, Commissioner Smith had directed the Sioux Agents to inform Indian leaders their people must return to their reservations by January 31, 1876, or be deemed hostile. But most off reservation Indians refused or were unable to abide by the order. On December 15, General Phillip Sheridan received orders to prepare to move against Indians failing to return to their reservations. On February 1, 1876, Interior Secretary Chandler wrote Secretary of War Belknap, "Said Indians are hereby turned over to the War Department for such action on the part of the Army as you may deem proper under the circumstances."[cxiv] Now a former black ops military intelligence remote viewer focused on a target envelope dated Montana, June 25, 1876.

McMoneagle – I have a sense that I am somewhere on the great northern plains in a place that is pre-dominantly rolling hills along a medium sized (Bighorn) **river, with a few ravines or erosion zones; in or near the eroded areas are a series of what appear to be ravines, these are filled with brush, small trees, and are used by smaller game as a place to live. I figure (based on military equipment and firearms) this is probably post-Civil War, or sometime around 1870, give or take a few years.**

This is an area of the Continental United States, which is still

looked upon as a territory of some kind, not part of a state. It is located in the North Central part of the United States, but does not seem to be mountainous. It is predominantly rolling grass-covered hills with trees now and then.

There is a large river to the Northwest (Yellowstone) which travels from the Northeast to the Southwest, and a smaller river or southern tributary off the larger river that drives downward through a flat area between the hills towards the Southeast (Little Big Horn).

There is heavy erosion in this area, which appears to come from large herds of animals that frequent or graze the area heavily. There is moderate rain year round and heavy snows during the winter. The size of the area as depicted with in the map attached is approximately 25 miles north to south and 30 miles east to west.

In 1876, the United States Army had orders to move the Great Plains tribes to designated Indian reservations. However, the Government effort was undermanned for this adversary in this territory. Without railroad or tactical field telegraph, troop dispersion became the rule. In the clutches of wagon train supply, U.S. military maneuvers were comparatively slow. Moreover, cavalry was less effective in the mountains. Yet, it was the only way to close with the quick and discerning American Indian.

For the army logistical concerns were paramount whereas for Indian war parties they hardly existed. For an infantry column to surprise a summer Indian campsite was difficult because of the Native American's superb scouting. In response, the military capitalized on the Indian's ancient Achilles heel. They employed rival tribes as scouts and guides. In previous 1870's campaigns, the U.S. Army used, "...Crow, Arikara, Osage, Shoshoni, and Apache scouts (who) proved indispensable in locating the objective and easing a command into striking position."[cxv]

McMoneagle – Indians with Custer – The "others" mixed with the soldier are also NA's, (Native Americans) **but from different tribal groups, some from the extreme east and northeast.**

G.A. Custer: *Inseparable from the Indian character...is his remarkable taciturnity* (silence), *his deep dissimilation, the perseverance with which he follows his plans of revenge or conquest, his concealment and apparent lack of curiosity, his stoical courage when in the power of his enemies, his cunning, his caution, and last but not least, the wonderful power and sublitude* (sublimation) *of his senses.*[cxvi]

In 1876, a converging columns strategy, emulating the army's successful 1874-75 Red River campaign, was again ordered out. That year General George Crook's (1828-1890) orders were to approach from the South, while Colonel John Gibbon (1827-1896) arrived from the Northwest.

Evidential Details

General Alfred Terry's force was to approach from the Northeast.

The 1876 campaign was upset by Chief Crazy Horse when General Crook was repulsed at the battle of the Rosebud.

But on June 17, Crook was stalemated by about 1000 Indians under Chief Crazy Horse on the Rosebud River. Having lost only nine soldiers, Crook was nonetheless forced to retreat south to his supply train. But the Native Americans had not brought up all their men and it is interesting to speculate how Cavalryman Custer would have handled that battlefield topography.

The Indians understood that non-reservation campsites would be destroyed and that this was dangerous for their families. But this also created problems for the army. The author of the Interior Department's *Little Bighorn National Park Handbook* summed it up. The problem with attacking an Indian village was that soldiers encountered women and children as they "...mingled with the fighting men, often participating in the fighting, and in the confusion and excitement of battle were difficult to identify as noncombatants."[cxvii] Accidental or not, this created casualties resulting in the death of loved ones and the longing for vengeance.

Now, for Seventh Cavalry, it was nearing the end of June, 1876 in Montana. The Sioux encamped in the Little Bighorn Valley had previously held a four-day Sun Dance ceremony in the Rosebud River valley. Their leader was Chief Sitting Bull. "It eventually became widely known that he was special, that his medicine (psychic ability) was good although he was not raised as a mystic."[cxviii]

Evidential Details

Hunkpapa Sioux Chief Sitting Bull (1831/4? - 1890)

    The Indian's Sun Dance ceremony required that a man undergo the excruciating pain of forcing sharp sticks sideways underneath the breast muscle along his rib cage. Rawhide ropes were then tied to these sticks. Amidst beating drums and burning sage, these men were lifted off the ground so they could "dance."

    According to accounts, Sitting Bull had fifty pieces of skin taken from his right and left arms in a torture sacrifice. He then danced for eighteen hours until he fainted. When revived, he spoke of warriors coming down on soldiers like grasshoppers and the soldiers falling. "Then the people rejoiced. They did not need a holy man to interpret Sitting Bull's vision—clearly it foretold of an attack on the camp by the soldiers, who would all be killed by the Indians. Even the most sophisticated Agency Indian present at the Sun Dance was impressed by Sitting Bull's performance and made into a believer."[cxix]

    "Although he is remembered as a holy man, a wise man, a chief, Sitting Bull had to earn his reputation first through many such courageous acts. He proved himself time and time again in his early manhood, leading raids and war parties against other tribes."[cxx]

Evidential Details

McMoneagle - Sitting Bull - Very professional, not only as a tactician but also as a strategic planner, as well as politically astute. He was probably a great warrior in his time, known for his tenacity in battle and fearlessness. At the time of this battle he was approximately 38 years of age, married, had two sons and a daughter, and was revered as not only a great leader, but also as a mystic, or one who could see the future.

He was however foolish in thinking that it (battle) would mean anything in the long run, and it probably resulted in the eventual loss of their lands, as well as their own massacre, which I have a sense came later. I believe he eventually made peace with the soldiers and was allowed to live out his own life as an old man. I do not believe this man died in battle or prison.

By June 19, 1876, Chiefs Sitting Bull and Crazy Horse had moved their people from the Rosebud riverbanks and the Wolf Mountains, to meadows along the Little Bighorn River. This was likely the largest Indian camp ever seen in North America. According to author Robert Utley, "They were numerous, united, confident, superbly led, emotionally charged to defend their homeland and freedom, and able, through design or good fortune, to catch their adversary in unfavorable tactical situations."[cxxi]

McMoneagle - There is a large encampment along the edge of the River... This camp is very large, essentially laid out with about 65 percent of the camp to the northeast, and about 35 percent to the southwest, only a very thin line of huts or Indian wigwams separating the two.

I get a strong sense that the main part of the camp is probably broken up into at least three primary groups, possibly a fourth which is not nearly as large as the other three. The smaller (southwest) portion of the camp is pre-dominantly made up of a single tribe or group of individuals who is led by a very great (that is famous) war leader.

I must add that my perception is strong that they were probably camped on both sides of the river. What also may complicate the matter is the numerous turns and tucks in the river as it winds through the area that may give the impression of being either side in many cases. The primary group might have been on the south side of the river, but they actually occupied both sides. My sense is that it is flat on both sides of the river, at least out to a few hundred yards.

At the time of targeting, there is a huge herd of horses, which are grazing down toward the "hashed area" near the smaller river. These horses are located within a half mile of the camp, and northeast

Evidential Details

of the camp. Most are hobbled, which would indicate that they are Native American horses. The hashed area is the general area of the encampment for the Native Americans.

This seems to be a very confusing target. I have a sense that there are numerous Native American Indians in this target, but am having considerable difficulty in figuring out a specific tribe, as there seems to be quite a mix of different tribal garb, as though a number of tribes have come together for some specific purpose. I suspect the purpose is probably war, as many of these Native Americans are wearing war paint, or at least their horses are.

The warriors are (also) wearing war paint and carrying weapons, so my impression is that they know they are about to come into contact with a military force. My sense is that they have known about the military force in the area for some time, and so they have been preparing for this encounter. The Native Americans involved are easily three times that estimated by any of the soldiers. I believe the reason for this is that no one ever saw the extent of the Native American encampment.

* * *

George Armstrong Custer was like a nineteenth century bare-knuckle boxer that took on all comers and refused to retire. Born on December 5, 1839 in Rumley, Ohio, what made him dazzle in the saddle was his contempt for authority – friend or foe. Raised in a staunchly Democratic family, he was the youngest General in the Civil War on either side. In 1863, he graduated last in his class from the West Point Military Academy. He then went on to lead the field in Civil War Cavalry operations. Always looking for a fight, he was rash with flash. By age 24, he had commanded more soldiers than all the braves of the Sioux Nations combined.

Robert Utley points out in his book *Cavalier in Buckskin*, that during the Civil War, Custer, "…by age twenty-five, had written a record of military exploits that few soldiers exhibit in a lifetime."[cxxii] "His generalship combined audacity, courage, leadership, judgment, composure, and an uncanny instinct for the critical moment and the action it demanded. He pressed the enemy closely and doggedly, charged at the right moment, deployed his units with skill, and applied personal leadership where and when most needed. Individually, he fought with a fury and tenacity astonishing to all who witnessed his feats of daring."[cxxiii]

According to author Stephen Budiansky: "But the war proved Custer was simply the greatest cavalry tactician of the Union Army, perhaps the greatest of either army North or South. The fame and rewards he gained were more than earned by not just his boldness and courage but his military acuity."[cxxiv]

After the Civil War, Custer was sent to western Kansas to protect track-laying crews. In 1871, he was ordered out to Kentucky where part of Seventh Cavalry was sent to South Carolina to tax moonshiners and suppress the Ku Klux Klan. In 1872, he hosted Russian Grand Duke Alexis on a Buffalo hunt. In 1874, he made his Black Hills Expedition. So, as we turn to the Little Big Horn Valley that afternoon in June, 1876 we can start to understand his mindset as he came upon the Indian encampment. Custer loved to fight, and it is on such that history has invariably converged. Our interest is Custer's last hours as told from United States Cavalry's point of view.

McMoneagle - Custer - Very professional, but prone to fits of egotistic arrogance. I get a sense that he probably thought of himself as better than he actually was. He was approximately 35 years of age and very young to be holding the rank he was holding.

The leader of Group Two (Custer) does not appear to be military by appearance, he could be a civilian.[17] **I get a very strong impression like he is thinking not so much like a soldier but more like a civilian as well. He is very astute from a political sense, but stupid militarily; like he is more of a politician than a soldier. I think he probably was well liked in the Washington DC circles but not within the Army. I have a sense when he was out west he felt he was out of the loop with things back east.**

G.A. Custer: *To many Officers service in the west amounts almost to social exile.*[cxxv]

There was reason for this. Sweethearts George and Elizabeth Bacon Custer were indeed liked in Washington. However, Custer's real introduction to Washington style politics came when he got into a jam with the Grant Administration that almost kept him off the battlefield. Custer testified in Congressional Hearings on behalf of Native Americans about Bureau of Indian Affairs corruption and illegal profiteering on treaty obligation goods. For a variety of reasons Custer's mixed attitude toward the American Indian is a noteworthy component of the man's time on earth.

A Cheyenne woman named Kate Bighead knew Custer on sight. There had been relations between him and her cousin Me-o-tzi stemming from a meeting in the spring of 1869. Me-o-tzi had fallen in love with Custer and reportedly turned down all other marriage offers claiming she was wait-

---

[17] That day Custer was out of uniform wearing a red tie, broad brimmed white hat and a buckskin pullover shirt fringed with colored porcupine quills.

Evidential Details

George Armstrong Custer in 1863. Out of West Point for one month, he took on JEB Stuart's veteran Confederate cavalry at Gettysburg. Custer fought an hour long, wildly pitched battle to a draw ensuring that Pickett's charge had no support. During the Civil War, he was considered an excellent divisional commander.

ing for Custer to return. The two had held hands during an Indian ceremony in which a Cheyenne woman spoke some solemn words to the effect Custer had taken Me-o-tzi as his wife. Whether the already married Custer under-

Evidential Details

Frederick Remington's *The Smoke Signal* (1905)
Strong, quick and fully integrated with nature, American
Indians used smoke signal communications that were seen for miles.

Evidential Details

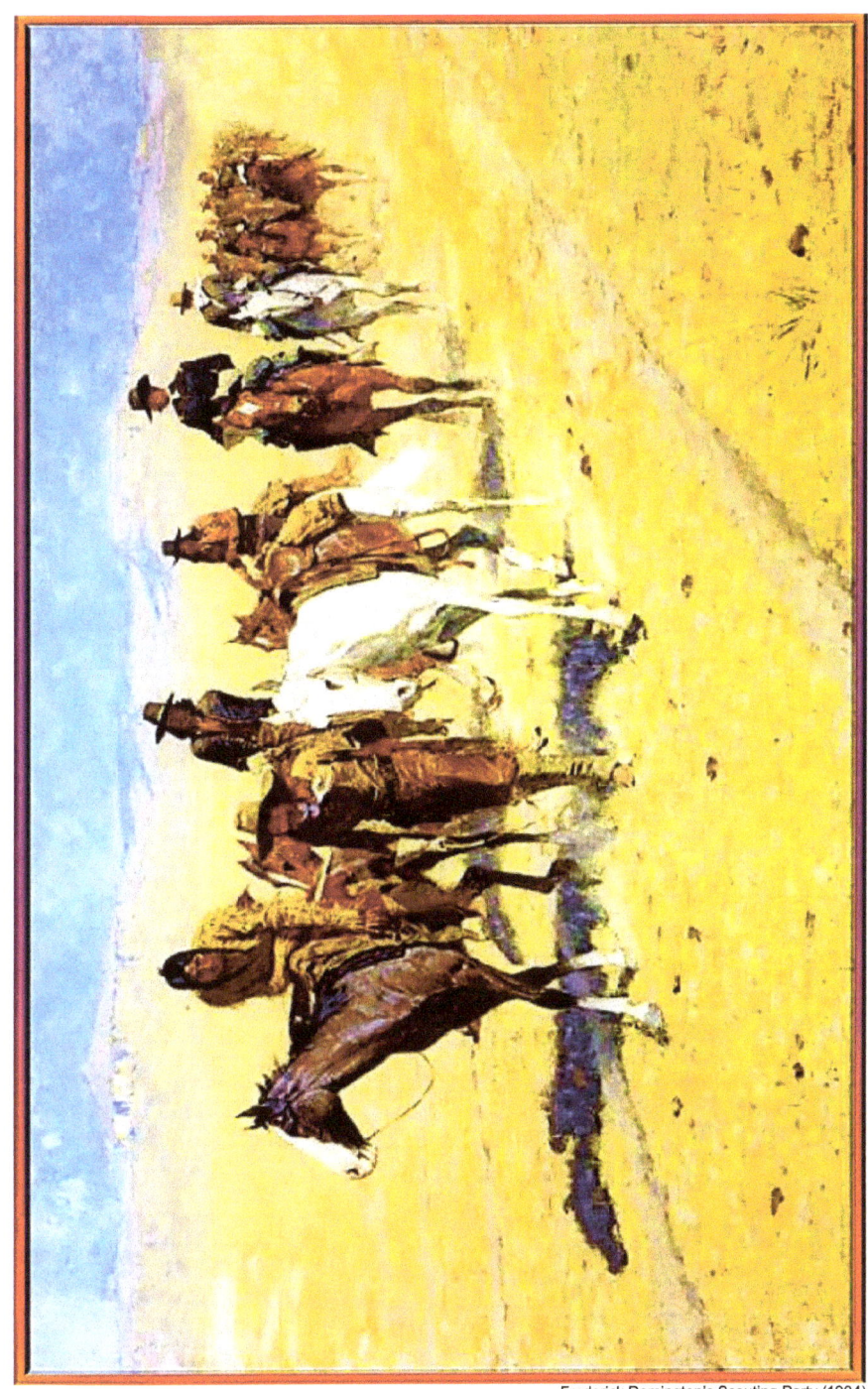

Frederick Remington's Scouting Party (1904)
Indian and civilian scouts did much of the tracking for the United States Army.

stood what he was doing is uncertain. However, nine months later Me-o-tzi bore Custer's baby girl who died. But Custer had been so taken by Me-o-tzi's beauty and cheerful personality he wrote in his book, *Life on the Plains*:

She was probably rather under than over twenty years of age. Added to the bright laughing eyes, a set of pearly teeth, and a rich complexion, her well-shaped head was crowned with a luxuriant growth of the most beautiful silken tresses, rivaling in color the blackness of the raven and extending, when allowed to fall loosely over her shoulders, to below her waist.[cxxvi]

Later I asked McMoneagle what he thought about Custer's Indian mindset.

McMoneagle - I don't think he much cared either way. He just wanted to get back to wine, women and song. Fighting was just his way of doing it.

In 1875, Custer had given leads to *New York Herald* newspaper reporter Ralph Meeker who then turned up at U.S. Army forts on the upper Missouri River as J.D. Thompson. Meeker reported on fraud and kickbacks regarding the granting of trading post concessions and Indian reservation sutler's licenses as well as at U.S. forts and military installations.

In the November, 1874 elections the Democratic Party regained control of the House of Representatives by a 169-109 margin and Chairmanships were re-assigned. After Meeker's corruption articles appeared in the papers the new Chairman, Heister Clymer, initiated a House War Department Expenditures Inquiry that reached into the Interior Department.

That Congressional Committee called Custer to testify about corruption in the Bureau of Indian Affairs. On March 15, 1876, he told what we knew about trading post licensing kickbacks. He appeared twice testifying honestly, perhaps naively, about reservation profiteering with a whistle blower's impact. Inadvertently, he emerged as a first person anti-Grant Administration witness. These proceedings became very sensitive when Grant's Interior Secretary was forced to resign in the emerging scandal.

Even more volatile was when the President's brother Orvil became a prosecution target for influence peddling. This was further aggravated when he wound up being the fall guy for Secretary of War William Worth Belknap and his cronies, who were now in an earnest attempt to stay out of prison on this Indian testimony.[18]

---

[18] The eight-year Presidential term limitation statutes did not become law until the ratification of the 22nd Amendment to the U.S. Constitution effective February 27, 1951. This was in response to Franklin D. Roosevelt's four presidential terms which, had he lived out his fourth, would have virtually extended from the November,1932 election to Harry Truman's presidency starting March 15, 1949.

Evidential Details

The "Large River" (top left) is the Big Horn and the "Small River" is the Little Big Horn. The "hashed area" is where the Indians were encamped.

Ultimately, Custer's statements helped force the resignation of Belknap who was the President's personal friend. The upshot was that this had helped bring needed reform to the Bureau of Indian Affairs. But in the Oval Office all this was seen to have advanced a cabinet level scandal that shut the door on Grant running for another term.

An enraged President demanded Custer report to the White House but then refused to receive him. Custer made three attempts to see the President and on the third waited five hours. Unable to get in, he visited both the Adjutant and Inspector Generals and then departed to Chicago on April 20. He was subsequently relieved of command and arrested for leaving Washington without having reported to the President. Then, as punishment for his testimony, Custer was forbidden to participate in the upcoming 1876 Yellowstone campaign.

But Custer wanted to be where the action was. Working behind the scenes, he succeeded in getting his commanding Officer Alfred H. Terry to

Evidential Details

countersign a letter requesting he be allowed to go on the expedition as a junior officer. Regarding the upcoming campaign, the correspondence from Brigadier General Terry to Lieutenant General Phillip Sheridan (1831-1888) read in part, *"...Lieutenant Colonel Custer's services would be very valuable with his regiment."*[cxxvii] But the attitude toward Custer's reinstatement was apparent in Sheridan's formerly classified communications to Washington D.C. It read in part:

I sincerely hope that if granted this time it may have sufficient effect to prevent him from again attempting to throw discredit upon his profession and his brother officers.[cxxviii]

From here, General Terry's requested went all the way to the top.

On May 8, 1876, Army Commander and Chief, William Tecumseh Sherman, (1820-1891) telegraphed General Terry indicating that if he wanted Custer, the President would withdraw his objections. He added:

Advise Custer to be prudent, not to take along any newspaper men, who always make mischief, and to abstain from personalities in the future.[cxxix]

The fallout from these cabinet level scandals meant that, for the election of 1876, the Democratic Party had the best chance to recapture the White House since the Civil War.

* * *

The year 1876 loomed large in the hearts of Americans because it was the Centennial celebration. It had been 100 years since the colonists had declared independence from Great Britain and fought a long and heroic revolutionary war. The economy was back from the panic of 1873, and pride filled the air as in many ways it was prelude to the Twentieth Century. For example, by 1876, milk was pasteurized and something called margarine was beginning to show up on kitchen tables whose legs increasingly stood on a new flooring called linoleum. The solar spectrum was photographed, and the library's Dewey Decimal system was introduced which cataloged Mark Twain's new book *Tom Sawyer*.

There was a Centennial World's Fair in Philadelphia to celebrate America's world-class ascendancy and the populace seemed in awe as they finally grasped the promise of electricity. In 1876, Thomas Edison (1847-1931) opened the world's first industrial laboratory in Menlo Park, New Jersey. He would go on to disassociate light from flame with his light bulb, which went on to transform the world.

At the fair was a gigantic electric dynamo that powered all the new inventions. This included an electric dental drill, tattoo machine, hair clippers, cigarette rolling machine, and a mass production power loom that halved clothing costs. The mimeograph and stenograph machines debuted and the first cathedral size electric organ was heard.

Melville Bissell (1834-1889) received a patent for the carpet sweeper, and Alexander Graham Bell (1847-1922) transmitted the first long distance conversation via a "Gramo-phone" wire from Cambridge to Boston, Massachusetts. Then preparations began for the world's first long distance telephone concert.

Nikola Tesla (1856-1943) was creating alternating current that went on to power the world. He was also experimenting with wireless electrical transmission.

George Westinghouse (1846-1914) patented the airbrakes that the Pullman Company used on their new refrigerated rail cars. This raised nutritional values with nationwide fresh meat and produce distribution.

Also available to try were all sorts of new food products like milk chocolate, ketchup, Hires Root Beer®, and Budweiser®. In addition, there were new farm combines that fed the Pillsbury® Company's new cold rolled wheat process.

In 1876 the first successful cannery opened and the first cantilever style bridge was completed. Patents were issued for the pipe wrench, barbed wire, petroleum jelly and the transformative typewriter. From France came the golden torch for the Statue of Liberty's construction.

Baltimore's Johns Hopkins Hospital opened and the next year new microscopes identified bacteria. Andrew Sill established Osteopathy as a medical science, and the first Dermatological treatise was published. Prudential Insurance® and the Eli Lilly Pharmaceutical Manufacturing Company® were founded along with the American Chemical Society.

It was also the beginning of modern sports. The first U.S. tennis tournament was played, and Churchill Downs opened in Louisville, Kentucky. The National Baseball League was founded and the baseball glove debuted. The U.S.A. took back the Americas Yachting Cup from Canada, and the first organized ice hockey games were hosted in Montreal.

So, this special July Fourth, 1876 celebration fed the American collective imagination as it congealed in the work of extending the world's first monarchy free constitutional democracy from the Atlantic to the Pacific Ocean. The press referred to the opening of the continent as America's Manifest Destiny. The country was doing well, and the populace wanted a safe transcontinental rail system as, "the United States continued its golden march toward wealth and power."[cxxx] The irresistible flow of consciousness was of a land united from "sea to shining sea." The people realized they had

Evidential Details

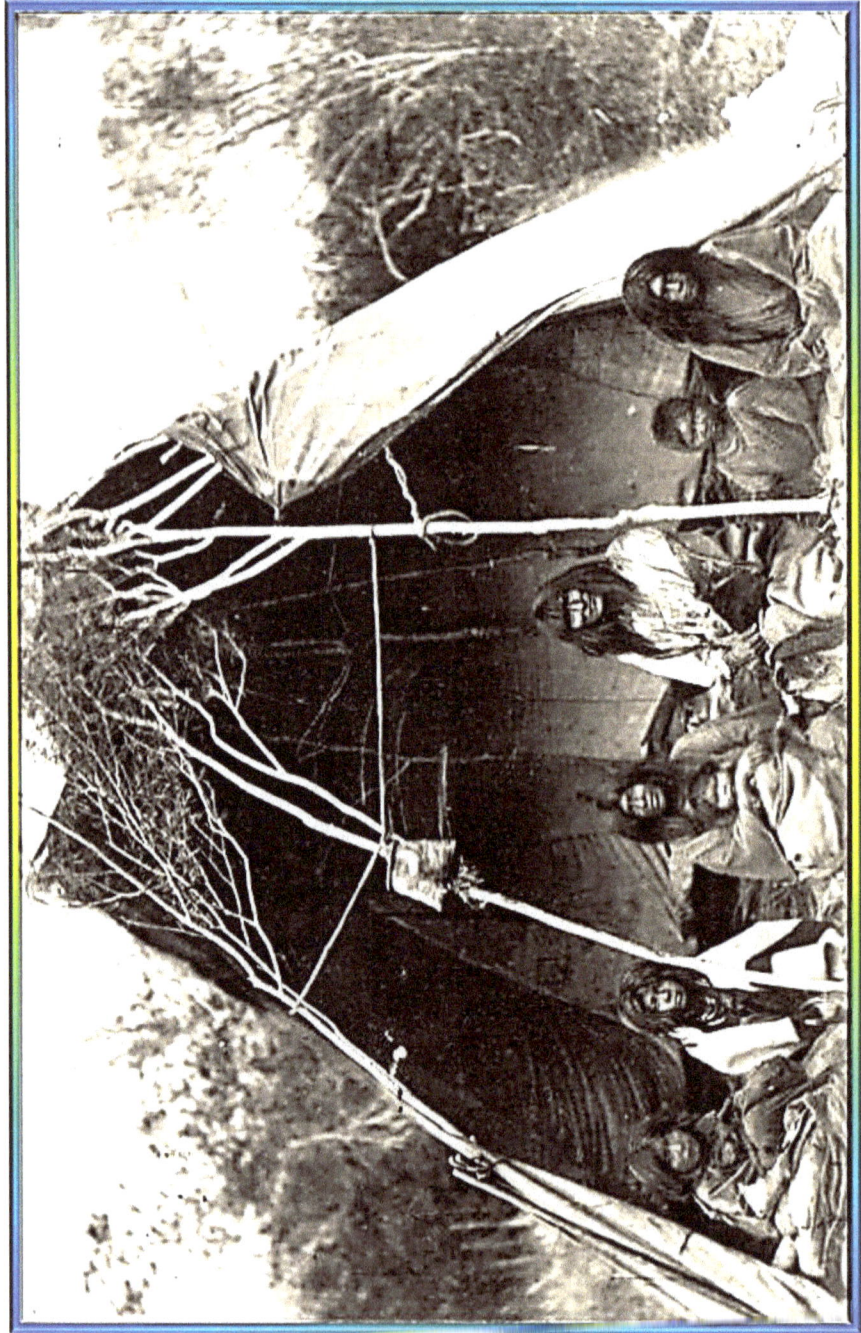

William Henry Jackson

Famous picture of a Bannock family of the Sheep Eater Tribe who allowed the press into their home on Medicine Lodge Creek, Idaho, in 1871. This image permits the historian to understand what men faced when returning home after an unsuccessful day of winter hunting.

Evidential Details

the technology and so it is inconceivable that any real "historian" could question why Custer's rout took the American public by surprise.

It was also an election year. Stung by his superiors, Custer needed to redeem himself. However, the positive publicity he received, coupled with openly mingling with anti-Grant Democrats, meant he was now considered a man of integrity willing to stand up and expose corruption even in the administration he served. So, in April, 1876, Custer had dinner with Senator Thomas F. Bayard (Delaware) and wealthy Hebrew banker, key campaign manager and former Chairman of the Democratic National Committee, August Belmont.

Belmont disliked New York Governor Tilden and was touting second term Senator Bayard as an alternative in that year's Democratic primary.[19] Either way the Democrats wanted Custer's star added to their roster. There was talk Custer could be a future Democratic candidate, receive a General's commission or maybe serve as Secretary of the Army in a Democratic Administration.

Another topic of conversation was that Custer had recently suffered his worst financial setback ever with the collapse of the Stevens Lode Silver Mine near Georgetown, Colorado. Back in 1871, Democratic Chairman Belmont had made the sizeable contribution of $15,000 to Custer's silver mining interests elevating the total investment to $35,000, which had now gone bust. So to make money, Custer had started to write his memoirs.[20]

But now, just before the 1876 Democratic Convention, loomed a campaign of different sort. A Custer victory would re-confirm him as a winner, hence an excellent high-level appointee. A contest between two very different cultures was now imminent.

* * *

As ordered, Colonel John Gibbon departed Fort Ellis, Bozeman, Montana on April 3, 1876, with just under 500 soldiers. Brigadier General Terry, and the now downgraded Lieutenant Colonel G. A. Custer, departed

---

[19] Samuel Tilden became the Democratic Party's presidential candidate in 1876. After the election, Tilden disputed the electoral vote count in what has been called the "stolen election." Remembered as the candidate who won a majority of the popular vote, he lost the Presidency when the Electoral Commission reversed three states on a decision not finalized until Feb 28, 1877. Former Brigadier General Rutherford B. Hayes was elected in a trade for a commitment to put a Southerner in the president's cabinet and remove Union troops from the South thereby ending the Civil War's Reconstruction era.

[20] Historical currency engines estimate that in 1876, $35,000 in 2014 currency was equal to about $766,860. Custer also received $10,000 ($219,100) from John Jacob Astor who died on the Titanic in April, 1912, $15,000 ($328,650) from August Belmont, and had likely invested $10,000 of his own money.

Evidential Details

Fort Abraham Lincoln, a few miles south of present day Bismarck, North Dakota on May 17. A deeply in love Libby Custer rode with her husband for three days before turning back. Remarkably, she had dark forebodings about this sortie even though there was no more clear and present danger than on previous Indian missions. Her premonition may have been from a dream. Four days before his death she wrote him:

<u>Libby Custer</u>: *I cannot but feel the greatest possible apprehensions for your safety on this dangerous scout.*[cxxxi]

<u>Sigmund Freud</u>: *There can, indeed, be no doubt that there are such things as prophetic dreams, in the sense that their content gives some sort of picture of the future;*[cxxxii]

Elizabeth Beacon Custer (1843 – 1934). Being the eldest daughter of a wealthy Michigan State Judge, Custer married the most proper and sought after girl in the county. She married a swashbuckling West Point Calvary General that had fallen in love with her. Rarely in history has an equivalently passionate love affair lasted from start to finish. Infertile, they considered adoption but Custer died too soon. Devastated, she devoted the rest of her life to his legacy. She was 33 when he died and lived on to an extraordinary 91 but never remarried. Her legacy was to write three books that provide a rare woman's account of life on the Western Plains.

Custer's rendezvous with destiny would take him 340 miles. Slightly ambiguous, the interpretation of his orders is an ongoing controversy because two words were later found to have been altered for the military hearings. It was not until the discovery of the original documents decades later that the correct wording was revealed, focusing interest on the commanding officer Alfred Terry.

On June 22, Terry issued his orders through Eighth Infantry Assistant Adjutant Captain Edward W. Smith, from their base camp at the mouth of the Rosebud River. On the one hand:

It is of course, impossible to give you any definite instructions in regard to this movement, and were it not possible to do so the Department Commander places too much confidence in your zeal, energy, and ability to wish to impose upon you precise orders which might hamper your action when nearly in contact with the enemy.

Evidential Details

On the other hand, regarding the possibility Custer should find the Indian's trail:

Should it be found...to turn towards the Little Horn (sic), *he* (General Terry) *thinks you should still proceed southward, perhaps as far as the head-waters of the Tongue* (River), *and then turn toward the Little Horn...*[cxxxiii]

Edgar S. Paxson (1909)
Seventh Cavalry Indian scouts returning with reconnaissance information.

These orders reaffirmed the convergence of forces strategy. But Custer was prepared to disregard any such timetable. And so it happened that at 9:00 p.m. on June 24, Crow scouts returned with news that they had discovered a large fresh pony trail west of their position headed toward the Little Bighorn Valley.

Evidential Details

Now Custer decided to move westward over the Rosebud Divide rather than swing around the mountains and approach from the South. Even though General Terry's command was 50 miles out of position, one can imagine a fighter like Custer ignoring that his scouts had just located the mother lode Indian causeway.

McMoneagle – Custer - My sense is that he was in direct violation of his orders from the Commander of Group One (General Terry). **The Group One commander was actually attempting to not only control him, but was also using him as a feeler, or patrol in strength. Bad idea at the time, given the numbers of Native Americans and the quality of their leader.**

He (Custer) **also thinks of the Native Americans as being quite backward and not understanding warfare, which is about as dumb a mistake as one could make. My sense is that he grossly underestimateed the strength of his enemy as well as his enemy's planning and execution ability. A lot of arrogance in this man, but I think most of his men know it too.**

<u>Feedback Question</u> – "Any idea how this guy could go from dead last in his class to lead the field in real combat, in which he wanted nothing more than to fight the best the enemy had?"

McMoneagle - They obviously used him to do the dirty work. As long as they praised him for it, he believed what they said about him. He simply did the nasty stuff and then blew it all out of proportion; e.g., kill a bunch of NA's (women and children) then claim he fought a pitched battle. When the NA's finally had enough, they brought in their best and wasted his butt. However...there were some who simply did their duty and saw no way out of it. I think they all pretty much knew it was only a matter of time till he got them killed.

Custer's Captain, Frederick Benteen, a fighter himself, disliked Custer. In the Civil War, he had been gallant in battles at Wilson's Creek, Pea Ridge and Vicksburg. Now third in command, Dutchman Benteen never liked reporting to a man five years his junior. And he detested what he considered a braggart's pretense. His failure to attempt to support Custer has always been suspect. He also disrespected the second in command Major Marcus Reno, who was terrified of Indians. General Terry did not like Custer either and did not even want to be in the field. Such were the underlying politics as this doomed litter of cavalrymen swung westward in what became a forced night march.

The next day, about fifteen miles out, veteran scout Mitch Boyer warned Custer that ahead lay the largest Indian concentration he had ever seen – anywhere. Custer's original intent was to attack at dawn on July 26.

Evidential Details

But his Crow and Arikara scouts returned advising a seven-brave Sioux scouting party had detected his approach. So, with only hearsay battlefield information, Custer moved his engagement timetable forward to that same afternoon.

George Armstrong Custer (1839-1876) taken at Memphis, Tennessee in 1873 – four years before his death.

Ohio Historical Society

Screened by trees along the river, Custer believed the dust swelling from the village was the Indians hurriedly breaking camp when they were actually rising to do battle. He became concerned that by disobeying orders, he would now be responsible for the Indians having all night to slip away. He ordered his men to move immediately. With only twelve companies of 40 to 50 men each, Custer outlined his plan. Seventh Calvary was to be split three ways in the face of this massive foe.[21]

Custer made his battalion assignments. Captain Benteen's orders were to make certain the Indians did not escape via a southerly route. He was given three companies (D, H, K) to move slowly into a reserve and blocking position. But at various times Benteen lagged from 30 to 80 minutes behind schedule.

McMoneagle – Benteen's forces - There is a force of combatants that are not NA's, but it is difficult to tell exactly what they are. There seems to be a mix of both military as well as non-military together. About 15 percent of the total, who seem to be about 10 percent soldiers and 90 percent other, (with 150 wagons they are) **...moving**

---

[21] In 1876, a fully manned Cavalry Company constituted 84 men with horses. At full strength, Seventh Cavalry would have consisted of 718 enlisted men. Each soldier was issued a Springfield single shot carbine with 100 rounds of ammunition and a colt revolver with 243 rounds.

Evidential Details

across the north within five miles of the camp, encircling to the southwest. In some cases they are operating separately from one another, in others they seem to be operating in concert with one another. Lots of shifting around.

Captain Frederick William Benteen (1834-1898)

At approximately 2:45 p.m., Major Marcus A. Reno was given three companies (A, G, M) to cross over the Little Bighorn River and attack the Indian village. According to Lieutenant E.S. Godfrey's statement, Custer's orders were for Reno to:

...move forward at as rapid a gait as he thought prudent, and charge the village afterward, and the whole outfit would support him.

The idea was to open a diversionary front giving Custer time to drive northwest toward the middle of the four-mile long Indian village. He would then strike with five companies (battalion) in the center/rear. Having ridden all night, his men and horses were tired, but Custer knew the Indians had discovered his forces and figured there was no time to lose before they scattered.

Custer and Reno rode along Reno Creek toward the village's southeast side. Reno then crossed the Little Bighorn River and opened his diversionary attack. At about 3:00 p.m. Custer wheeled his men up the bluffs and galloped at approximately 7.5 mph north-west uphill across the river from the Indian city.

Native American numbers have always been controversial. Custer's briefings indicated approximately 800 combatants were to be expected. This would put him at a 3.5 to 1 disadvantage.

Evidential Details

McMoneagle – Indian Numbers - Within this encampment, there are approximately 4,800 to 5,500 people consisting of approximately 2,800 warrior age Native Americans, 2,400 women, and approximately 300 to 350 children or lesser-aged Native Americans. The weather is not cool, nor is it very hot. I get a sense that it is sunny, light cloud cover, and probably about 65 to 70 degrees (18.3 – 21°), **once the sun is well up.**

This is in contrast to misstatements about the day being brutally hot. The average high in Miles City, MT on June 25 is 80°F (26.6°C).

Major Marcus Albert Reno (1834 –1889) was the Senior Officer reporting to Custer.

The die was cast. The men were on the move. There would be no turning back. Seven of twelve companies, and the supply train would not be available to Custer. His 232 men would face approximately 2800 warriors at approximately 12 to 1 odds.

* * *

About 35 miles north, General Terry's command crept cautiously along the Yellowstone River's south side. McMoneagle denoted this American military force as Group One.

McMoneagle – Group One - On the opposite side of things, the military group is made of approximately 1,000 men.

This was a good estimate. The actual numbers were 1,140 including civilian wagon teamsters; 925 were soldiers.

McMoneagle – Group One/General Terry - I have a sense he (Terry) *hated* **his subordinate, the other commander** (Custer). **I have a**

sense that he felt he was a rogue soldier, only out for his own glory and perhaps with a political bent. He knew he would probably get into trouble when he allowed him to patrol to the south, but did so anyway. He also knew that he would never fulfill any direct order he gave him. So, *he was not about to come to the rescue.* He *deliberately delayed* by pretending not to understand the precarious situation the man was in, and taking his time to gather his forces to march to the area as a relief.

Hated Custer! Deliberate delay! It is clear General Terry was not in a position to support Custer that day. But the new research thread became was there was any evidence of a deliberate failure to support armed forces under his command leading to a massacre. A closer look at General Terry was clearly in order.

Alfred H. Terry was an attorney before the Civil War and was not fit for field command as was understood by Custer. During the war he had been appointed a Colonel in the Connecticut Infantry in September, 1861. His claim to fame was that after a nearly sixty-ship naval bombardment under Rear Admiral David Porter, Terry's 8,000 men defeated Fort Fisher's 1,500 Confederates under Colonel William Lamb on January 15, 1865.

This largely overlooked second assault in North Carolina was successful, in part, due to the failures of Lamb's thoroughly incompetent senior officer Braxton Bragg, who refused to send the reinforcements at his disposal. As a result, the South's last import/export gateway was shut down 85 days before General Lee's surrender. After the war, Terry received a Congressional congratulation and decided to pursue his legal career in the military.

Mild mannered, nothing is heard of Terry until he was selected for the Yellowstone campaign of 1876. A man of culture, speaking several languages, he was a tidy bachelor coasting on a General's paycheck. With conciliatory demeanor, he appreciated the fine arts and literature and held the respect of his peers. But he had not seen military action since the first quarter of 1865. Wealthy, this 49-year-old had no interest in field command, and had no experience fighting Indians which is why he countersigned the letter requesting Custer be reinstated. Terry needed protection.

McMoneagle – General Terry - A basic down to earth leader of men with absolutely no imaginative ability, or great desire to excel at what he was doing. He was essentially a "lifer" waiting for his retirement. He had absolutely no desire to make contact with the enemy, but was simply following his orders at the time.

Why the high command had chosen Alfred Terry to lead a mission against the dangerous Sioux and Cheyenne is difficult to understand. Grant, Sherman and Sheridan had sent an attorney! Perceived as pleasant Judge

Evidential Details

Advocate legal counsel, he was ordered out before being too old to take the field. His ability to work with everyone led to insubordination from both Custer and Reno.

Intriguingly, his field diary was not released until 92 years after the battle (1968), with a quickly revised second edition released in 1970. Those revisions are important. So, were there any evidential details about his indifference towards Custer? Upon review, the Little Big Horn days of his diary seemed very irregular.

Custer's commanding Officer in the field, Brigadier General Alfred Howe Terry (1827-1890). His elbow on a thick book, he was a calm and soft-spoken man of intellectual pursuits.

For example, one paragraph in the diary ends with the words: "(*rest of entry too light to be legible on xerox copy*)". If you believe this, the historian is left wondering why this part of the page was not simply typed out. More atypical publishing activity involved deleted information that obstructs critical timeline research, such as: *Reached camp at ------*."

Also, key words parenthetically marked "(*illegible*)" are used liberally. For example, during the second day of battle his diary reads, *Indians in parties of* (illegible) *or less* (illegible).[cxxxiv] How is it that deciphering Terry's penmanship presented no problem for the publisher except on key words? There were also many entries stating, *"Page torn in half,"* which leaves historians wondering why, when and by whom?

In what was an unexpected research turn, one would think any publisher would have taken some effort to decipher these alleged illegible

Evidential Details

words. All told, there are 15 dashed-out words, 9 pages torn in half and 14 words marked "illegible", among 20 vital paperback pages. Terry's diary has been rendered incomplete, hence historically unsatisfactory. In a post remote viewing environment, it gives the distinct impression of a cover-up and leaves the historian wanting the 1968 version or the original papers.

McMoneagle - Terry - Group one is moving across the north of the camp location and is at a considerable distance, perhaps twenty miles. There are at least one major line of hills and a couple small rivers dividing them off from the actual locale of the coming battle. They are moving almost due west at a slow walk and stopping to rest frequently while their scouts search ahead for the primary concentration of Native Americans. They are way too far to the north and east however to make contact; about 40 percent of the total (Seventh Cavalry)**, who seem to be about 85 percent soldiers and 15 percent other.**

Subsequent research showed McMoneagle was correct. On the battle day, Terry's "**slow walk**" was as follows:

<u>General Terry</u> - June 25: *Started 5:30* (a.m.). *1st halt 6:35. A(dvanced) 6:55. Gained summit and halted at 7:55. Advanced 8:35. Halt 9:40. S(tart) 10. H(alt) 10:50 for* (a gun) *battery which had broken a pole. S 11:20. H 12:20. Started 12:45 and reached Big Horn at about half past one.*[cxxxv] Two hours and 15 minutes of rest time before 1:30 p.m.

Extremely apprehensive about Indians and his personal safety, Terry got to the mouth of the Bighorn River, (Bighorn, MT.) approximately 90 minutes before Reno kicked off his abortive charge. In his telegram to Chicago, Terry estimated it was 29 to 30 miles between his forces and Custer's. But, even with a day documented to be full of rest periods, he reported:

<u>Terry Telegram</u> - *The men were very weary and daylight was fading. The column was therefore halted for the night...*"[cxxxvi]

<u>Feedback Question</u>: "It has to do with the Group One commander deliberately delaying his relief of the battlefield by taking his time. I wanted to ask, if this guy's attitude was ever uncovered, from a military standpoint do you think it would have been grounds for a court martial?"

McMoneagle – Could have been grounds for CM back then, but then I get the impression that just about everyone (militarily) **hated the arrogant leader so no one really cared.**

Both Gibbon and Custer had quality Crow scouts. Terry's intent was to have the army perform an enemy encirclement to prevent a large breakout. Custer had the Cavalry and Gibbon had Gatling gun equipped infantry that could stop any northern retreat. If the Indians escaped to the South, General Crook was thought to be in position. As Seventh Cavalry approached, both opponents were confident. However, the Ree scouts began to realize that Custer's command were dead men riding.

<u>General Terry</u>: *Here he found a village of almost unexampled extent, and at once attacked it with that portion of his force which was immediately available.*[cxxxvii]

Unfortunately for American arms, Major Reno was also deathly afraid of Indians. Just after 3:00 p.m., he moved his 112 troopers two miles toward the village though terrain suited to cavalry operations. But, as he approached the massive Indian village, he decided not to launch the ordered assault. Instead, Reno had his men dismounted. They formed into a skirmish line and commenced lobbing bullets long range into the village. A small Sioux Indian force challenged Reno at about 3:20 p.m., just as Custer approached the Cedar Coulee {large ravine).

McMoneagle – Major Reno – ...makes initial contact with the Native Americans just southeast of their encampment at approximately ½-mile distance. They are grossly out-numbered even by the small party of Native Americans moving south along the river. (Initially his) **...men actually only lost one man** (Indian scout Bloody Knife), **then turned and ran to the North. They break contact and immediately begin to turn back toward the main part of the Group Two column. However, this is thwarted by the Native Americans who are flanking them to the east, turning the soldiers scouting party due north, where they make a run for high ground.**

As the Indians moved on Reno's left, he withdrew east northeast into a thicket of cottonwood trees on the Little Bighorn banks just after 3:30 p.m. This fight lasted about twenty minutes until a terrified Reno decided to withdraw approximately one mile to a passable ford where his troops could get back across the river.

Reno then led a stampede without making sure his retreat orders had even been passed along. As a result, sixteen soldiers wound up stranded on the wrong side of the river. Reno's action was so inconsequential the Indians did not even bother to follow-up although a few did stay to keep the stranded troopers pinned down. The approach, skirmish, and retreat took about one hour. Reno lost four officers and half his men.

McMoneagle – Captain Benteen - ...on the other hand has swung far to the south in order to make what appears to be a very broad sweep or flanking action across the face of the smaller river. (His troops will) **...more than likely be joined after...** (Reno) **encounters the smaller segment of the NA camp and sees the size of it. I envision them being chased back to Group Two where they will seek protection. I get**

Evidential Details

Reno's diversionary "attack"

a sense that some of the Native American scouts (White Swan, Half Yellow Face and Curley) with this group were able to get away and survived to talk about the incident.

McMoneagle - (Custer with Companies C, E, F, I , L} - ...hears the gunfire from (Reno's) **initial contact and moves rapidly forward to engage the enemy, which they do slightly southeast of the smaller river.** Custer's force numbered, "13 officers, 193 enlisted men and 4 others for a total of 210."[cxxxviii]

As depicted in the attachment, Group Two [Custer] has moved west to the river and then turned north to follow the eastern side of the river northward. This group has been broken down into two additional smaller groups – Group Three [Scouts] and Group Four [Companies E and F]. Looking at attachment three you will see two X's, which identify the actual location of two battles.

Group three is a forward scout unit, made up of what appears to be six soldiers and four Native Americans. They are approximately two miles out in front of the main Group Two column (Custer), **also riding along the eastern side of the smaller river** (Little Big Horn).

With Reno engaged, Custer pressed on northwest along the river's northern side. As events developed, he started to realize the village size and sent Sergeant Daniel Kanipe back some three miles to tell Benteen to bring the pack train forward.

At just after 4:00 p.m. Custer was informed Reno was in retreat. Custer dispatched another courier. Then, in an effort to support Reno and buy time for Benteen's reinforcements to come up, Custer divided his forces again. To divert pressure on Reno, he sent Captain Yates, with two companies, to feint an immediate attack across the river. At about 4:20 p.m. these men arrived at the riverbank where they were immediately opposed by the Cheyenne. The Native Americans now knew Custer's general location.

McMoneagle – Sub-Group Two (Yates) **- is moving down toward the eastern edge of the NA camp and towards the river. They are moving due south toward the Native American Camp. The NA group about to engage Group Two is much larger. They outnumber Group Two by about four to one. Although the movement implies they know where the Native Americans are located, in reality they don't.**

They are moving on the supposition that is probably the most likely place in which they will find them, since that is where they have been known to camp before. In reality, the commander of Group Two (Custer) **seems to have grossly underestimated the size of the encampment, or the numbers of warriors present there. This,** (sub) **Group Two**

Evidential Details

The afternoon troop movements of Lt. Colonel Custer, Major Reno and Captain Benteen culminating in the last stand battle (top left).

Evidential Details

is essentially riding into a shit storm and has no idea that it's about to happen.

Initially when contact was made down by the river it was head on, but the odds were so over-whelming they broke contact (at least tried to) and moved toward high ground. Had they made a run for it, they would have probably survived, or at least some of them would have. They were assaulted from all sides.

As for the battle, the (Yates) **soldiers give a good accounting. They initially started the contact in a charge but that was quickly routed, so they actually went on the defensive very early in the game. Perhaps ten minutes in. I think they did this when they clearly saw the numbers of Native Americans that were showing up to do battle. So they went on the defensive when they made the run for high ground, having to actually fight their way to it from the river. We call this a tactical retreat under fire.**

Yates attempted to disengage up Deep Coulee toward a rendezvous with Custer's main force, who had also started to engage the Indians. Their reunion took place at about 4:45 p.m. Custer also sent a company forward to scout against the possibility Indians may have crossed the river upstream on what will become the Federal right.

The soldiers fell back to Calhoun Hill where they tried to stand their ground as the Indians fought on foot up through the ravine system. Then Indians under Lame White Man rose to the attack. Then Gall's braves. Federal troops were forced back into what is known as the Keogh sector. Here the first hand-to-hand combat took place. By the time, Custer's troops fell back to Last Stand Hill there would only be about 102 remaining.

McMoneagle - **As the soldiers die, they fall back farther and farther toward the center of their respective hilltop, eventually being overrun by Native Americans. Group Two is essentially standing their ground to the east northeast of the NA encampment. They will be systematically encircled and pinned down on a small hill with their backs to two ravines.**

More Native Americans arrive quickly, which drives the flow of battle almost due north away from the encampment to the same high ground now being occupied. This is actually a tactical error on the part of the Commander since he is easily surrounded there by over-whelming force. A very large group of NA's (about sixty percent of the entire NA force) (Crazy Horse) **is moving to engage Group Two.**

When they (Custer's men) **took higher ground, they killed their horses and formed a protective group of two circles. Believe he** (Custer) **gave the order to shoot the horses and use them for cover.**

Evidential Details

Day One. Little Big Horn Battlefield looking north. The Indian city was in the green on both sides of the river. Seventh Calvary came in from the right (east) side. The last stand was made close to the red dot (top center) where the National Park Buildings are today. Also visible are the ravine systems the Indians used.

Evidential Details

Chief Gall, 36, (1840-1893) led the attack on Custer's left. He would fight the longest and lose the most that day. One of his wives and children were killed by another Indian tribe.

They shoot their horses and use them as defensive positions from which to hide and shoot from behind. He took cover behind his and his Sergeant's horse there. The Sergeant (Robert Hughes) was killed up near the outer perimeter in the first twenty minutes.

Lying behind their horses, they fought the Native Americans as they were being encircled. The Native Americans essentially charged them both on horseback as well as tried to work their way in on foot using the low places in the ground. They also sent in teams of men vis-à-vis the trenches (ravines) **behind the high ground. Eventually the soldiers seemed to have been just overwhelmed.**

I have the sense that he (Custer) **was in the front edge of his men initially then moved more to the apex of the hill so that everyone could see him. Toward the last ten minutes, there were no orders being given other than keep firing 'till they exhausted their ammunition. At least three attempts are made to get someone off the hill to ride for help but they are cut down within a hundred meters of the hilltops.**

The NA's held in reserve (Crazy Horse) **will join the first group of NA's who encounter Group Two. This will actually take place after the first major entanglement between Group Two and the original NA Group** (Gall) **sent to meet them.**

Two Eagles stated there was a firm stand on "Custer Hill" and that this group had been *the most stubborn*.[cxxxix] Hollow Horn Bear said the soldiers had resisted "*hard*" in the Custer Hill sector. But without topographical information, Custer had occupied a position where he could not win. Two ravines that protected the enemy's advance were in his rear.

These horse bones give the historian an idea about the dismounted trooper's scant protection. The field of fire can be seen along with a loop in the Little Big Horn River (blue arrow). The size of the enemy is shown by five dots as they approached rifle range (yellow arrow). This is likely Custer's last view as he moved forward from the rear into an overwhelming enemy.

McMoneagle - Almost no fighting seems to be taking place on horseback. It all seems to be on the ground. Both Native Americans as well as soldiers are fighting with rifles. Of course, the Native Americans are also fighting with some bows and arrows. Over half the soldiers are wounded at least twice before falling from their wounds. At least a quarter of the soldiers are struck by bullets or arrows three or more times before dying. They will run out of ammunition.

Feedback Question: "Did there come a time the arrogant commander knew the fight was lost? Any thoughts on his actions?"

McMoneagle - He knew he had made a serious tactical error as soon as he saw the numbers he was faced with. He actually thought he

Evidential Details

could still duke it out and deal with it. I think for the first thirty minutes or so, on the high ground he felt he could just muscle his way through it, just like he had in the past. But around forty minutes in, he realized he was going to die there along with his men. I think he deliberately exposed himself so that he would die early on.

When he knew that he was going to die anyway, he decided to go out in a blaze of glory. This guy was screwed up in the head actually. Very arrogant and very politically minded. Looking for his place in the history books.

McMoneagle RV Art – Evidential Details ©2000
The previously ill defined, Cemetery Ridge battle is shown as 'Secondary battle location'. (left) "NA's escape" shows how Custer's Indian scouts departed as the battle started. Crazy Horse's flanking movement is entitled "**NA's close left flank**".

Most gunfights are hornet's nests. Nothing likes having bullets cracking all around your ears and ricocheting off of things. The trick, if there is one, is to ignore them and think your way through the fight

Evidential Details

Reverse angle looking south. With a field of archers in their front and Gall on the left, Crazy Horse's men came up the ravine about 35-40 minutes later and hit Seventh Cavalry's rear at which point, Custer then moved to the front of his troops.

Evidential Details

McMoneagle RV Art – Evidential Details ©2000
Group One is Terry's command. The "Larger Group" is Custer on Last Stand Hill. The 'Smaller Unit' (center left) is Lt. Smith scouting party with the newspaperman.

and do whatever is necessary to stay alive and keep as many of your guys alive as you can. You soon reach the understanding that when you are supposed to die, you will, nothing you can do about it. Up until that moment, your job is just that - your job. You do what you've got to do just to stay alive and get the mission done.

In actuality (they) fought it out for approximately one hour and forty minutes, give or take five minutes. In fact, many of the men were fighting with as many as two or three arrows in them. I get a sense that it takes a while to die from an arrow wound, especially when it doesn't strike a vulnerable place.

Me-o-tzi's cousin, the Cheyenne woman Kate Bighead, was in the village that day. She knew Custer and was apparently the only woman to cross the river to witness the battle in progress. Now, seven years after Custer's relations with Me-o-tzi she watched his sector go down. About the weapons used against Seventh Cavalry, she wrote:

But a rain of arrows from thousands of Indian bows, and kept up for a long time, would hit many soldiers and their horses by falling and sticking into their heads or their backs.[cxl]

McMoneagle - Custer's death - The Commander dies within the first for-

Evidential Details

Last Stand Hill. The soldier's positions were previously unknown. Crazy Horse hit the Command Post from behind, sending Custer forward. **McMoneagle – The numbers 5,2,2,5 indicate the numbers of people** (soldiers) **and where they died.**

Evidential Details

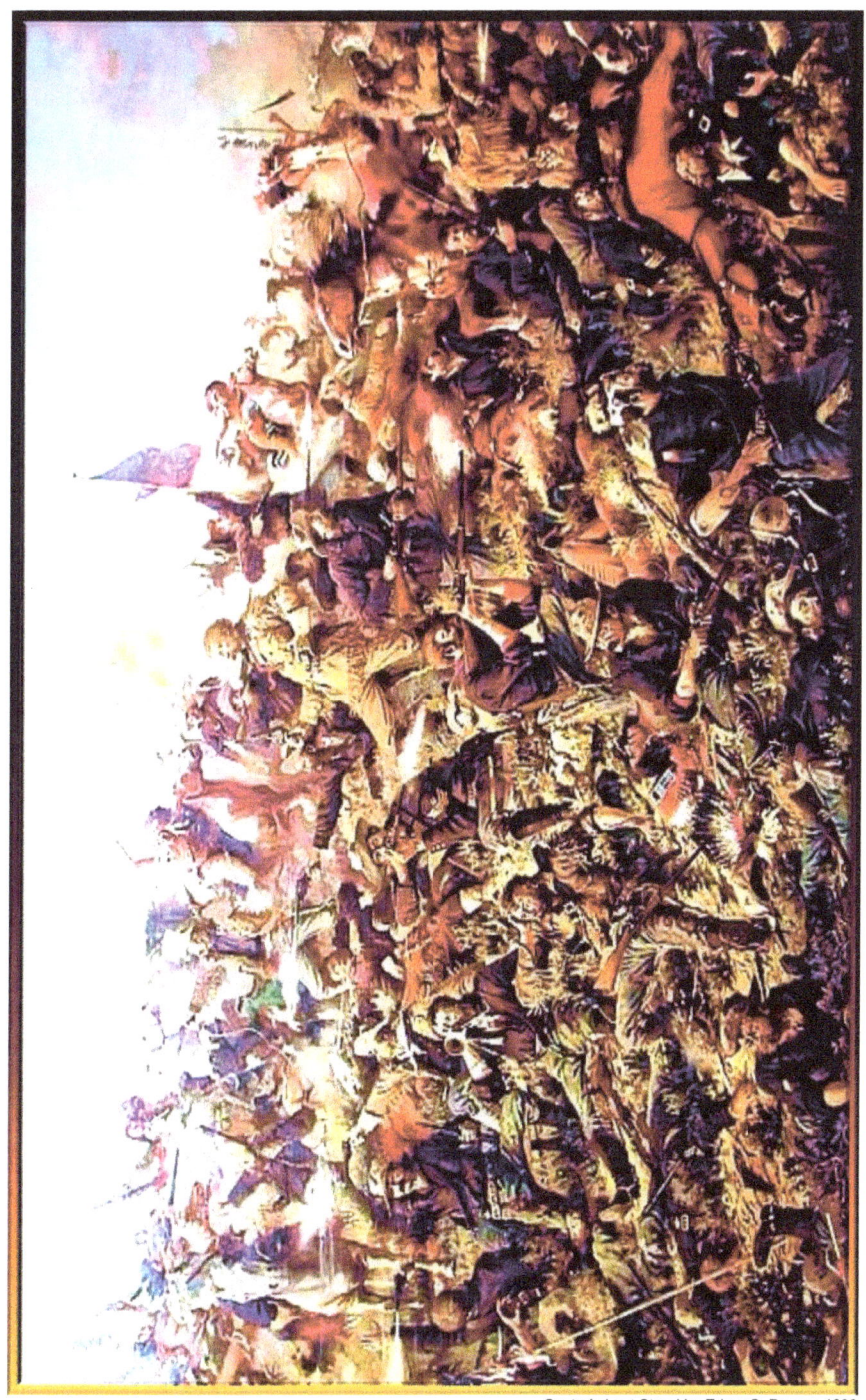

Custer's Last Stand by Edgar S. Paxson 1899
With Custer in the middle, this famous 6 x 9 foot
painting attempts to recreate the chaos of being overrun.

ty-five minutes of the battle, having been struck by an arrow through the left eye socket. He was wounded at least twice before he died by arrow. He fired at them 'till he was hit by the arrow, then dropped to his knees and continued to yell at his men to fight. I do not believe any of the wounds except the eyeshot would have actually killed him. After he was struck by the other arrows, he simply fell over and died but probably very slowly over a ten to fifteen minute period.

His internalized regrets were that he couldn't live out his life and experience what he knew his life was here for - get very political aspirations here. I also have a sense that he had a girl or sweetheart somewhere, which he was suddenly aware that he would not see again. I think he had some regret about not spending more time with her.

He did understand that he was about to die and had a very great internal struggle with himself about dying in a grand way. He wanted to be seen as courageous, but understood that there probably wouldn't be any survivors to tell about it. So, in the end, he was simply stripped of most of his arrogance and died righteously along with his other men. He had no fear once he got past that point of realization. He then fought as best he could until death took him.

I think he truly regretted his life - at least the way he had lived it 'till that point. There is great clarity that always comes with death upon someone and I think he had that at the end. How he truly loved those around him, but had never really told them (the men he was with). He was using a set of side-loaded colt revolvers, which had custom grips of some kind of bone.

But Custer was reputed to be carrying self-cocking English Bulldog pistols, not colt revolvers. I went back with this information.

McMoneagle - In the heat of battle, especially back when there were no automatics (handguns), I cannot see someone fighting an entire fight with their own single weapon. Sure, as long as there are only short duration skirmishes, and there is time to reload the weapon, they would continue to fight with the same weapon.

But in an extended engagement, where you are being overwhelmed you fire your weapon till it is empty and then go to the sword (throwing the hand gun away), or you pick up what's available, which would be another gun that a dead man has dropped. Stopping to reload would be out of the question while being overrun. I can tell you, all the survivors were inside a circle less than 60 feet across and standing back to back. I don't know anyone who ended the fight with their own weapon. In fact, some of the survivors were holding bloody rocks in their hands.

Evidential Details

McMoneagle RV Art – Evidential Details ©2000

<u>Question</u>: Is it possible to draw a picture of the commander from maybe 25 feet away just before he died? This would be an important picture if it is possible.
McMoneagle - Yes I can do that.

Evidential Details

Floating real time window. Custer's face as he realizes he is not going to make it.

McMoneagle RV Art – Evidential Details ©2000

<u>G. A. Custer</u> - *Surely no race of men, not even the famous Cossacks, could display more wonderful skill and feats of horsemanship than the Indian warrior on his native plains. The Indian warrior is capable of assuming positions on his pony, the latter at full speed, which no one but an Indian could maintain for a single moment without being thrown to the ground.*[cxli]

With Custer down, the soldiers had no leader and were bunched as a circular archery target. The men could not easily hit moving targets firing bullets and arrows from virtually 360 degrees. Eventually each man experienced the sudden intense electrical shock of a penetrating arrow from nowhere.

Hundreds of stabbing non-mortal puncture wounds took the men's senses to a painful dread mode. The sight of blood effected alarm as penetration ache mounted. Death struggle sounds with fresh blood smell reinforced their fear. This mortal stress intensified the flailing fight work as the sense of no way out mounted. Of just over 100 men, about 45 would die with Custer. Then, as their numbers dwindled, they somehow made a decision to abandon the hill and make a desperate run for what is known as the South Skirmish Line

McMoneagle - South Skirmish Line - A few will attempt to escape down these ravines (washes), but these ravines will also be used by the NA's to gain access to the group dug in on the hill. Any

attempt to use the ravines for cover is essentially suicide for the soldiers, as they have been quickly occupied by Native Americans, who are using them to get in close to the hilltops.

The ravine was about 15 feet deep and 20 feet wide at that point. Wounded and desperately fatigued from an all-night ride, the men somehow fled pell-mell through a 610-meter gauntlet of shrieking death. Only about half (28) made it through the wild, frenzied maniac panic to the ravine. Now surrounded in a rugged deep walled gully, already partially occupied by the enemy, the men never had a chance. A few even failed to fire or attempt to reload.

They looked as if they were drunk; their brain's visual spatial realities dulled by a helplessly impending violent death having affected their motor function. Detached, some died with fully loaded pistols in their belts as they beheld the surreal spectacle of war-painted men jumping down on their person to proudly initiate the deathblow.

It was the senselessness of resistance that was so at odds with soldiering. Then, the deep burn of a red-hot bone-crunching bullet into your body. A couple steps to the side as their screaming intensified. Suddenly touched by the enemy your cranium explodes on tomahawk stone. Complete fatigue as you drop to one knee. Then, gasping incapacitation, as a large hunting blade from the side rips deep up into the rib cage penetrating heart and lungs and introducing indescribable chest pain. Fibrillation and cardiovascular spasm. Another hatchet blow to the side of the head opens the skull and the last exhale. It would be fascinating to have digital graphics of the last image each soldier's brain processed.

McMoneagle – They were just overwhelmed. The NA's won. Kicked their asses. There is only one survivor, that being a message carrier...

As the battle opened, the last man out alive, H Company's bugler John Martini, carried the second message to Captain Benteen. It read: "*Benteen: Come on. Big village. Be quick. Bring packs.* W.W. Cooke. P.S. *Bring Packs.*"[cxlii] In a letter dated Brooklyn New York, on March 24, 1909, Martini wrote:

When I left Custer he was about 200 yards from his command. I could see the Indian village, but not Major Reno's command. ...it was about three miles from where I left Custer to where I met Benteen. I was about half an hour, going at a gallop.[cxliii]

There are many versions as to how Custer died. As time went on, and interview money became available for "firsthand accounts," embellishments were added. Sitting Bull himself related to a New York *Herald* news-

Evidential Details

Charles Kuhlman Collection

South Skirmish Line. Not realizing this ravine was full of Indians, 28 soldiers made a final desperate rush for trenching protection. Notice the white grave markers.

paperman an apocryphal 1877 account as relayed to him by braves from the Hunkpapa tribe:

Sitting Bull: *Up there where the last fight took place, where the last stand was made, the Long Hair stood like a sheaf of corn with all the ears fallen around him.*
Reporter: "Not wounded?
Sitting Bull: *No.*
Reporter: "How many stood by him?
Sitting Bull: *A few.*
Reporter: "When did he fall?
Sitting Bull: *He killed a man when he fell. He laughed.*
Reporter: "You mean he cried out.
Sitting Bull: *No, he laughed. He had fired his last shot.*[cxliv]
When asked by a reporter if the men had fought to the last:
Sitting Bull: *Every man, so far as my people could see. There were no cowards on either side.*[cxlv]
Chief Rain-In-The-Face: *I had always thought that white men were cowards, but I had great respect for them after.*[cxlvi]

As for the intellectualization of the battle, it has been asked how Seventh Cavalry wound up in this situation. James Fox Jr. gives his take on the American Calvary:

Therefore, using measures employed today, we can fairly say that tactical cohesion in the Custer regiment was substandard... The introduction of new recruits at inopportune times probably diluted the reservoir of esprit de corp and unit pride within the regiment. Moreover, cohesion and stability suffered because of a lack of unanimity in subscribing to abstract societal values. In launching its campaign, the regiment was there-fore ill prepared normatively and technically, and as a body it entered battle acutely susceptible — especially when faced with an unconventional enemy — to agents that provoke dissolution of moral unity.[cxlvii]

We agree unit pride and shared societal values are essential in any successful military and that the degrading of these influences need to forcefully opposed. I sent this quote to McMoneagle.

McMoneagle - What he has done is mixed apples, oranges and pears. This is rhetoric from a guy that has never been shot at. Ground truth - to the combat soldier it all goes by the wayside when you are going to die.

Whoever is intellectualizing the battle is missing a very large point. That is not the way it happens in combat. When the bullets fly and the crap hits the fan, it brings people together. This is especially true when there is no hope and the unit is essentially being anni-

hilated. It becomes a "pack in the face of death." All differences of race, religion, sexual preference, background, rank, age, etc., dissolve around the issue that you are sharing death together. Men come together, they become almost matter of fact in their actions, and they generally give good accounting of themselves. There may be an exception to that rule, but they are far and few between, and always singular in example; e.g., a man may collapse in terror, freeze, or run. But, in all my experiences in twenty years in the Army, I've never seen that happen a single time, which really tells you something about soldiers - especially American soldiers.

McMoneagle earned the U.S. Army's Gallantry Cross with Palm for his actions in the Vietnam War.

Feedback Question: "Can you comment on fear factor of the defeated. Do you consider them to have been a tactically cohesive unit?"

McMoneagle - This is what's very surprising. They fought to the end as a cohesive unit. They didn't break, they didn't panic, and they didn't give up. At the end, I have a sense that some of them put bullets into their buddies who were severely wounded in order to protect them from agonizing death. But, these were very brave men. They knew, because of the odds, that they were probably going to die and gave a very good accounting of themselves. Very brave men.

That tactical disintegration took place early on is untrue. Nor was Seventh Cavalry technically ill prepared. Native Americans are to be credited for having defeated a stubborn foe, as it appears only about one in ten braves had a rifle. The estimated number of rifles available was approximately 375 for 2800 Indians meaning over 2,400, or 86%, used the bow.

An estimated 150 Indians died. "Which brings up another mystery surrounding the Battle of the Little Bighorn: Where was Sitting Bull during the fight?"[cxlviii] No one knew, but there were three odd versions of Sitting Bull's whereabouts. They include that he was moving the women and children away from the action; he was making medicine in his tepee; and that he was riding at the front of his warriors in the battle. So, during the feedback phase I asked if he had taken part in the battle.

McMoneagle - Not directly. He stood on an adjoining hill and directed the action of his men. He only came into the battle at the very last when there only a few of the soldiers left fighting. It was more of a triumphant ride to claim his victory. I have a sense that he was actually somewhat saddened by the whole affair, as if he knew it was the end to something important to him.

That evening General Terry had a relaxed Officer's dinner ("*the onions were divine*") and slept securely. The next day:

Evidential Details

<u>General Terry</u>: *The scouts were sent out at half past 4 in the morning of the 26th. They soon discovered three Indians, who were at first supposed to be Sioux, but, when overtaken they proved to be Crows, who had been with General Custer. They brought the first intelligence of the battle. Their story was not credited.*[cxlix]

Myles Keogh

George Yates

Thomas Custer – younger brother

James Calhoun

Four of Custer's Officers killed that day.

Evidential Details

McMoneagle – Group One (Terry) - **hasn't a clue to what's going on and is essentially not going to be engaged in the primary fight. Group One is contacted but responds by sending Group Two** (Custer) **a message to fall back and regroup; a message Group Two never gets.**

In the revised diary, Terry does not mention this directly. But scouts were sent forward who probably carried his message. He then ordered General Gibbon's men forward as a buffer. Terry held his position in reserve to support Gibbon's force if needed.

General Terry: *During the afternoon efforts were made to send scouts through to what was supposed to be General Custer's position, to obtain information of the condition of affairs; but those who were sent out were driven back by parties of Indians, who, in increasing numbers, were seen hovering in General Gibbon's front.*[cl]

McMoneagle - Even though at least two Native American Scouts escape the debacle following the initial contact near the river, no help is ever sent to aid Group Two as by then Group One (Terry) **understands the odds and time have run out. I believe the Group One Commander probably sends a message advising the Group Two Commander to fall back and not to fully engage the Native Americans – but the Group One Commander has no idea that the numbers of Native Americans there are what they are.**

Until this research, Native Americans were the only ones to recount what happened and numerous accounts have been documented. As the battlefield analysis continues, Robert Utley summed up Indian recollections:

Indian testimony is difficult to use. It is personal, episodic, and maddeningly detached from time and space or sequence and topography. It suffers from a language barrier often aggravated by incompetent interpreters, from the cultural gulf between the questioner and respondent and from the assumptions of the interviewer not always in accord with reality.[cli]

McMoneagle - The entire battle (including Reno) **takes approximately two and one half-hours, plus or minus ten minutes** (3:00-5:30).

Direct from the battlefield, Custer's scouts advised Gibbon's Cavalry of the situation, and Terry chose not to move. His troops arrived on the battlefield approximately 40 hours after his command was notified. Though Custer's troops could not have been relieved, the second day's fight should have been.

General Terry – Last Stand Hill: *It is marked by the remains of his officers and men and the bodies of his horses, some of them dotted along the path, others heaped in ravines and upon knolls, where halts appear to have been made. There is abundant evidence that a gallant resistance was offered by the troops, but that they were beset on all sides by overpowering numbers.*^{clii}

In 1991, a comprehensive metal detector forensic dig time/motion battlefield study was published.

McMoneagle - Following the battle, many of the bodies of the soldiers are stripped of their clothing, valuables, and these bodies are mutilated with knives and hatchets. This is not a vindictive action, but an action to guarantee they will not return again to these Native American lands. It is also done, because the Native Americans understand this gives fear to their enemies.[22]

"It appears probable that the majority of the troopers were still alive but more or less helplessly wounded when resistance ceased and that many were finished off with massive crushing blows to the head."[cliii] "The mutilation of the dead was a customary cultural expression of victory over the vanquished for the Indian participants of the battle and should not be interpreted as specific to the Custer battle."[cliv] As it turns out, corpse mutilation was rife and many have wondered why. Eyewitness Scout George Herendeen (aka Bad Heart, 1845-1920) recounted:

Hordes of squaws and old gray haired Indians were roaming the battlefield howling like mad. The squaws had stone mallets and mashed in the heads of the dead and wounded. Many were gashed with knives and some had their noses and other members cut off. The heads of four white soldiers were found in the Sioux camp that had been severed from the trunks, but the bodies could not be found on the battlefield or in the village. Our men (American soldiers) *did not kill any squaws, but the Ree Indians did.*[clv]

As for Custer, historians write that his body was stripped but not mutilated like the rest. Nonetheless, they said there was, "a gash cut in his right thigh, a finger digit removed, and an arrow shot into the genital area; also the eardrums had been punctured by a squaw's sewing awl."[clvi]

Mass corpse mutilations offend African, Spanish, Oriental and European sensibilities. The reason for this was the Indian's view of the afterlife, which was distinct from other world cultures. As recounted by Chief Red Cloud:

The idea of the spirit land is that it is a physical paradise; but we enter upon its mysteries in just the condition we hold when we die. In the Indian paradise every physical taste or longing is promptly met... In the light of this idea, those tortured bodies had a new significance. With the muscles and arms cut out, the victim could not pull a bow string or a trigger; with other

---

[22] The Seventh Cavalry used the Model 1873 Springfield Carbine and Colt Revolver. Both were .45 caliber weapons. Bullets and shell casings recovered from the battlefield suggest the Indians used twenty-eight different types of firearms. Forensics analysis determined the most common were the 55 Winchester and Henry Model 1866 repeater.

Evidential Details

Red Horse drawing circa1893
Native American depiction of Seventh Cavalry soldiers after the battle.

muscles gone, he could not put foot in a stirrup or stoop to drink; so that, while every sense was in agony for relief from hunger or thirst, there could be no relief at all.[clvii]

McMoneagle – Post (first day) **battle activities were actually much longer than battle activities. Post activities lasted about two, to two and a half hours. Mostly it dealt with tending to their own wounded and stripping the dead bodies and horses of their enemy.**

The Custer engagement was over, but not the Battle of the Little Big Horn. By now Benteen and Reno had combined their forces and were digging in some 3.5 miles away on what became known as Reno Hill.

McMoneagle – Reno and Benteen - ...occupy a higher and lower hilltop, which are side-by-side where they fight it out to the end. In fact, some of the Native Americans had to move to the fight...after they had disposed of the Group Two men. Water plays a major role in the outcome, both the lack of it (day two)**, and the ability to ford the river without horses.** (They)**...were in a much more protected spot. There is no attempt to send for help. I get a sense they were actually in a ravine and had the walls of the ravine to protect them. They were also not attacked by such overwhelming odds.** (These) **...men actually went the distance on time.**

Seventh Cavalry's 350 soldiers and civilians fought until sundown and then most of the next day. Custer's battalion had been annihilated but, omitted in America's paltry historical education system is that Reno and Benteen fought the Indians to a draw the next day. Captain Benteen actually led a charge into a threatening Indian position.

With lopsided numbers and a water shortage, Seventh Cavalry's determined resistance forced the Indians into a siege that had melded into a draw before day's end. The Indians then abandoned the field as their scouts confirmed Colonel Gibbon's southbound approach.

On June 27, 1876 the day dawned bright and clear as Gibbon's soldiers moved on to what was to become a National Battlefield Park at about 11 a.m. Lieutenant Bradley was the first to reach the entrenched survivors over on Reno Hill. He brought news of what had happened on Last Stand Hill. And as they spoke, the Democratic Convention was opening to great fanfare in St. Louis, Missouri.

Denouncers swear Custer was out-generaled by the Indians. But the Tribes had not planned a battle, they had responded to an attack. The truth is that a poorly informed G.A. Custer jumped into enormous odds and wound up on the worst possible terrain. Custer's battalion was flanked, from behind and on four sides, while hotly engaged. With a 24 hour hold, Colonel Gibbon's men could have been nearby.

Evidential Details

Stalemate. Day two in the Battle of the Little Big Horn. With an attack on all sides, Captain Benteen's counterattack is shown lower right.

Evidential Details

Thinking it through, with these odds the Indian tribes simply took care of business. Consider that 137 football players defeat 11, or 62 basketball players out play 5 on the same court. Would the victorious team be cited for vastly superior coaching?

The true military achievement is that an intertribal Native American force did a superb job using a ravine system to strike the enemy with a quadruple envelopment. The Indians had attacked across a flowing water obstruction, wet, uphill. In the process, they eliminated a skilled veteran commander and his entire force comprising just over 50% of Seventh Cavalry. Nonetheless, while the Little Big Horn's first afternoon was a tremendously successful large skirmish, it only partially advanced the Indian's strategic needs. In comparison with other "great" command scenarios, Chiefs Sitting Bull, Gall, and Crazy Horse needed to defeat the soldiers on Reno Hill. These three Companies of dismounted Cavalry were an obstacle to Native American northbound lines of communications.

Then the Indians needed to protect their immense village by moving north to check Commanders Gibbon and Terry. Gibbon's Gatling gun enabled forces would have been a tough fight, but General Terry's defensive mentality could have resulted in a withdrawal spelling another success for the Indians.

In the end, military analysts agreed that due to the well documented Indian scatter and re-group strategy, Custer had no choice but to attack or potentially face accusations of timidity in the face of the enemy.

In 1873, Custer had won on the Yellowstone River with a 5 to 1 disadvantage. But, assuming 100 Indians had died before the final clash on Last Stand Hill, the odds were a little more than 12.5 to 1 by the time Custer's 210 men sustained the throw weight of at least 2700 Indians. And the American Indian was the ultimate asymmetrical enemy.

There were seven body counts, all with a slightly different number. By the end of the day, they settled on 214. On June 28 the men were buried - many where they were found. That same day Alfred Terry sent a telegram from his *"Camp on the Little Horn."*

General Terry: *The removal will occupy three or four days, as the marches must be short.*[clviii]

With the completion of the battlefield clean up, Terry moved north and set-up a depot close to the mouth of the Big Horn River. His July 2nd telegram to General Sheridan in Chicago read:

General Terry: *I have brought down the troops to this point. They arrived tonight. They need refitting, particularly in the matter of transpor-tation, before starting again.*[clix]

On August 1, six companies of the 22nd Infantry reported to Terry

Evidential Details

under Lieutenant Colonel E.S. Otis. The next day six more companies arrived commanded by Colonel Nelson A. Miles. The Cavalry Officer replacing Custer was Major Brisbin. One can only imagine what Alfred Terry thought as he rode the train back to St. Paul, Minnesota, realizing he had to explain what many believe was the single most significant defeat in U.S. military history.

Aftermath

General Terry's U.S. Seventh Cavalry suffered a 52% casualty rate. Because of what emerged as the failed Yellowstone campaign of 1876, Colonel Nelson A. Miles replaced Terry in October at the fort known today as Miles City, Montana.

One year later to the day, General Phil Sheridan left Chicago, Illinois to visit the Little Big Horn Battlefield. Custer's officers were then removed to be reinterred, except for Lieutenant John Crittenden, whose father wanted his son's body to remain.

On the battle's fifth anniversary a granite memorial was erected listing all the soldiers and scouts names. Underneath lay bones that were collected and buried in a long trench near the top of Custer Hill. In 1890, gravestones were placed approximately where individual soldiers fell although there will always be controversy as to their accuracy.

As for Chief Crazy Horse, "He was slightly below medium height and remained rather thin, weighting only about one hundred forty pounds. His color was deepening, but he was still of a lighter complexion than his comrades. His hair was light and long hanging below his waist when combed out; he almost always wore it in braids. His idiosyncrasies had hardened into habits."[clx]

****

Chief Crazy Horse (1840-1877) refused to have his picture taken believing photography stole a man's soul. While many claimant's photographs have been unmasked, no other efforts have him real time in what to date remains history's only accurate rendering.

****

After the battle, the charismatic leader became involved in a tribal leadership struggle with Chief Spotted Tail over issues that included the discontinuance of the Sun Dance ceremonies. Cautious, Crazy Horse rejected an offer to take the same trip to Washington, D.C. that Chief Red Cloud (1822 - 1909) had taken in 1870 to meet with both Ely Parker (1828 -

Evidential Details

McMoneagle RV Art – Evidential Details ©2000

Evidential Details

1895) and President Grant. His plan to meet and then kill his old adversary, Brigadier General Crook, at Camp Robinson, was exposed by a member of his own scouting group who was also Red Cloud's cousin.

Finally, Crazy Horse agreed to ride into Fort Sheridan amid a 40+ Indian escort assigned, "...to take care of him and prevent his escape."[clxi] He had come to state his case to U.S. Military authorities, but instead they escorted him to the blockhouse. Once inside, he realized he was in a jail and attempted to leave. A struggle ensued in the doorway with Little Big Man. Plenty Wolves grabbed the revolver Crazy Horse had under a waistband blanket.

Crazy Horse drew his hunting knife. Struggling with Little Big Man, he broke out into the yard and was finally bayoneted twice by a fort guard trying to break-up the knife fight. The surgeon brought him to the Adjutant's office and administered morphine for his pain. With his father at his side, Crazy Horse died at about 11:40 p.m. on September 5, 1877

After the battle, Chief Sitting Bull refused to report to the Great Sioux Reservation taking his people to Canada in 1877. But things did not go well, and he finally rode into Fort Buford to surrender at noon on July 19, 1881. In the mid-1880's he travelled one year as a featured star in Buffalo Bill's 30 year running (1883-1913) Wild West Show. He and Annie Oakley were the star attractions. With fascinated respect the public flocked to get a look at the great Sioux Chief that had defeated Custer.

On December 15, 1890, Sitting Bull was killed outside his home near Fort Yates when a supporter took a shot at a Native American Reservation Policemen who had come to take him into custody. Fighting broke out and Sitting Bull was shot immediately - once in the chest by Bull Head, and then in the back of the skull by Red Tomahawk. When it was over, twelve lay dead including Sitting Bull's son Crow Foot. The Indians scalped Sitting Bull, and beat his face "into jelly". His final resting place has, over the years, been turned into a controversy.

Chief Gall died curiously on December 5, 1893 - Custer's birthday. Why he was wounded is unclear, but he apparently died while in the healing process. His wounds had been re-opened when he fell out of a moving wagon. And what about Custer?

McMoneagle - The Commander is not mutilated however, but allowed to lie on the battlefield where he died, fully dressed, but stripped of weapons. His body was pretty evident among the others. He was the one dressed strangely -- with a pullover buckskin coat, decorated with porcupine quills of different dyed colors. I also think he was wearing a western hat that had a decorative scarf or something tied around it. He had very long, dirty blond (light brown) hair, pulled back

in a ponytail and tied with rawhide.

The AI's (American Indians) **all knew him on sight, or at least had excellent descriptions of him from other AI's who did know him on sight. When they discovered the body, they moved it away from the others to a place higher on the hill (or point of the hill), and then simply dug a hole and buried him. Out of honor (or maybe fear of his spirit) they did not strip the body or take anything off of it, except his weapons. The burial took place within half an hour of the battle.**

McMoneagle's account of Custer's burial is in complete contrast to the historical record. Supposedly, Custer's corpse was left on the battlefield with twelve other officers. The next summer, a burial detail retrieved these remains for proper internment back east. But they only brought seven to ten coffins (historically unclear) for the exhumations. Eleven officers bones were said to have been placed in the available boxes. Loaded on-board the riverboat *Fletcher*, these remains were taken down the Missouri River to Fort Leavenworth, Kansas.

As best as could be reconstructed, Custer, and his brother Tom, were buried by a detail comprised of Sgt. John Ryan of Company M along with two corporals and a private James Seaver. The Custer brothers were to have been buried side by side. The grave was only about 18 inches deep and was marked with a travois. But, when the burial details returned the next year, the recovery efforts were complicated by two-foot tall prairie grass. And some have had reservations about the whole scenario.

Familiarity with the problems of visually identifying the dead in mass-disaster situations and consideration of the bodies when they were found leads the authors to question the validity of some of the identifications made by the original crews. The positive identification of skeletal remains of the eleven officers and two civilians exhumed from the site for reburial elsewhere is also questionable. This is particularly true in the case of George Custer's exhumation, where the description of the grave and its contents are at odds with the account of the original burial.[clxii]

Feedback Question – "I wanted to ask if you were able to determine how the body of the arrogant leader was moved?"

McMoneagle – Not sure now that I worked it, that they moved the body that far. I think they buried it within about thirty meters of where he died. But, they did not desecrate the body for some reason, possibly because they appreciated his valour. He was moved to the highest point of the hill -- which was outside the ring of horses. He was buried with his feet facing West (setting Sun). He was buried in a shallow grave -- about three feet. I believe he was buried with all of his weapons, except his handguns, and these were taken by the chief of

Evidential Details

the tribe. There is something about his shirt that is different from the shirts the other men were wearing. I think if remnants can be found of his shirt in a grave, that would be the identifying part.

So the Indians buried Custer's unmutilated remains in the following manner:

- Within thirty minutes after the battle;
- Buried three feet deep outside the ring of horses;
- At the highest point on Last Stand Hill;
- Feet facing West;
- With a buckskin shirt, decorated with porcupine quills.

Burial crew uncertainty, coupled with McMoneagle's information, makes it more than 51% likely that the body in New York's West Point Military Academy graveyard is not Custer. This presents as the perfect opportunity for remote viewing feedback through DNA testing. So, if the decision was yours, would you order an exhumation?

And so it came to pass that as June's late sun descended into dusk, the greatest Indian village that may have ever graced the North American sky moved toward the Bighorn Mountains. Smoldering campfire smoke mingled with trail dust sunbeams creating a soft sunset haze that screened their immense exodus. And just four days later, with its motto being *Nothing Without Providence*, Colorado became the 38th State.

I must say I shall regret to see the (Civil) *war's end. I would be willing, yes glad, to see a battle every day during my life.*

George Armstrong Custer

Shakespeare: *These violent delights have violent ends. And in their triumph die, like fire and powder, Which as they kiss consume.*

Evidential Details

Credentials

JOSEPH W. MCMONEAGLE, CW2, US Army, Ret., KCStS
Owner/Executive Director of
Intuitive Intelligence Applications, Inc.

Mr. McMoneagle has over 45 years of professional expertise in research and development, in numerous multi-level technical systems, the paranormal, and the social sciences. Experience includes: experimental protocol design, collection and evaluation of statistical information, prototype design and testing, Automatic Data Processing equipment and technology interface, management, and data systems analysis for mainframe, mini-mainframe, and desktop computer systems supporting information collection and analysis for intelligence purposes.

He is currently owner and Executive Director of Intuitive Intelligence Applications, Inc., which has provided support to multiple research facilities and corporations with a full range of collection applications using Anomalous Cognition (AC) in the production of original and cutting edge information. He is a full time Research Associate with The Laboratories for Fundamental Research, Cognitive Sciences Laboratory, Palo Alto, California, where he has provided consulting support to research and development in remote viewing for 16+ years. As a consultant to SRI-International and Science Applications International Corporation, Inc. from 1984 through 1995, he participated in protocol design, statistical information collection, R&D evaluations, as well as thousands of remote viewing trials in support of both experimental research and active intelligence operations for what is now known as Project STARGATE. He is well versed with developmental theory, methods of application, and current training technologies for remote viewing, as currently applied under strict laboratory controls and oversight.

During his career, Mr. McMoneagle has provided professional intelligence and creative/innovative informational support to the Central Intelligence Agency, Defense Intelligence Agency, National Security Agency, Drug Enforcement Agency, Secret Service, Federal Bureau of Investigation, United States Customs, the National Security Council, most major commands within the Department of Defense, and hundreds of other individuals, companies, and corporations. He is the only one who has successfully demonstrated his ability more than two dozen times, by doing a live remote viewing, double-blind and under controls while on-camera for national networks/labs in four countries.

Evidential Details

Mr. McMoneagle has also been responsible for his Military Occupational Specialty at Army Headquarters level, to include control and management of both manned and unmanned sites within the Continental United States, and overseas. He was responsible for all tactical and strategic equipment tasking, including aircraft and vehicles, development of new and current technology, planning, support and maintenance, funding, training, and personnel. He has performed responsibly in international and intra-service negotiations and agreements in support of six national level intelligence agencies, and has acted as a direct consultant to the Commanding General, United States Army Intelligence and Security Command (INSCOM), Washington D.C., as well as the Army Chief of Staff for Intelligence (ACSI), Pentagon.

Other employment has included, Assistant to the Security Officer for a multi-billion dollar overseas intelligence facility, with responsibilities that included physical plant communications, personnel, and technology security; as well as counter-terrorist and counter-intelligence operations. He has served as the Detachment Commander at two remote intelligence collection sites overseas, providing field intelligence collection, analysis and reporting at theater, region, country, and city levels. He has also served on an Air and Sea Rescue team, in Long Range Reconnaissance, as a Quick Reaction Strike Force team leader, and rifleman. He has earned 28 military decorations and numerous awards, to include a *Legion of Merit* for his AC support to the Nation's Intelligence Community, and he holds the rank of Knight Chevalier in the Order of St. Stanislaus.

Interview Clarification

Question: Generally speaking, how much…information should be given a viewer in operations / applications?

Joseph McMoneagle: None. Zero. What you can do if the target requires a response or a description of an individual, you can say, "*Describe the individual at* (whatever location)" and the location needs to be hidden (would be a number, for instance). If you were targeting let's say a church, and there was an individual in that church, the church would be coded as say, "location A1". It would then say, "*Describe individual at location A1.*"

Under no condition can you give any information that is directly pertinent to the target. There is never any front-loading. The reason for this is because the entire concept of remote viewing is that an individual is forced, has no choice, but to use their psi ability to answer the requirement. Any info that is given in any way, or form, modifies that response in a way that removes / reduces the probability of accuracy.

Evidential Details

Human Use

Remote Viewing research sometimes involves input from different sources as in the application of the Army's Human Use Policies that were developed to protect soldiers from experimental harm.

"In February 1979, the General Counsel, the Army's top lawyer, declared [the early on Remote Viewing Program called] *Grill Flame activities constitute Human Use*." The Unit, "…was in the middle of the [authorization] process in March 1979 when the Human Use determination was reversed by the Army's Surgeon General's Human Use Subjects Research Review Board. Their decision…trumped the Army General Counsel's ruling…"

"On November 20, the Surgeon General's board changed its mind and decided that *Grill Flame* did indeed involve Human Use. It took until February 1, 1982 to get final approval from the Secretary of the Army to continue operations."[23]

New candidates were then issued a warning by a Major General before being accepted into the super-secret 902nd Intelligence Unit.

"Among other things, they noted that if he joined the project, he would be exposed to psychic phenomena at a level and with a frequency that most people had never experienced before. As a result, he might change in certain ways. Ultimately, no harm should come to him, but he might have a new perspective on himself, his marriage, the universe. In a sense, he might become a new man, and a new husband."

The candidate and his wife were advised to talk, "…this over before they made the final commitment to go to Fort Meade." [24]

THE 1973 REMOTE VIEWING PROBE OF THE PLANET JUPITER'S DISCOVERED RING

(The Planet Jupiter remote viewing) Experiment #46 lay obscure between 1974 and 1979. No continuing attempt was made to feedback other of its categories, and the SRI (Stanford Research Institute) work progressed along more immediately fruitful (confirmational) lines.

(Six years later) The 1979 (Voyager 2) scientific discovery and (the July 9, 1979) confirmation of the (Jupiter's) Jovian Ring came as one of the larger shocks - and surprises -- in astronomical history.

---

[23] Smith, Paul H., *Reading the Enemy's Mind – Inside Star Gate, America's Psychic Espionage Program*; Tor Non-fiction, 2005; p. 118
[24] Schnabel, Jim, *Remote Viewers: The Secret History of America's Psychic Spies*; Dell Non-Fiction, 1997, p. 270

Evidential Details

A Chinese Encounter

The United States is not the only nation to study and use Remote Viewing. Below is a narrative allowing enthusiasts and skeptics alike a rare look at life inside the Unit during the middle 1980's.

The first time it happened was right after [Major] General Stubblebine had briefed me on the project and said that I would be contacted. The next week I was working mid-shift, and one of the afternoons, I lay down for a nap. In that nap, I had a really shallow and lame dream about something I can't remember now. But at one point, right over the top of that dream there was what appeared to be a semi-translucent visual of three people.

One was a very respectable, businesslike slender man in a suit. A second was a very burly, stocky man, also in a suit, and with a very "Texas farmer" face. The third was an...oriental girl... (I find it impossible to tell the age of oriental women). She was following along behind the two men and watching.

The men came up to me and talked about something, but I couldn't hear them. The girl was standing behind the two men, listening. The faces were very clear. Clear enough that when the two men actually came to [the INSCOM[1] Base in Augsburg [Germany] to interview me, I recognized them immediately. I could have picked them out of a crowd on the sidewalk. I didn't think anything of the fact that the girl wasn't with them. It would have been odd to have her on a military trip overseas. I thought she was probably someone in the unit.

Months later, when I got to the unit, she wasn't there. I asked about her and neither the director nor Joe [McMoneagle] (the two men who came to interview me) knew who I was talking about. I figured that it was just an AOL (STRAY CAT)[2] and blew it off.

About a year later, I was doing a practice target. The target was a museum at Arizona State University (I didn't know that, I only had numbers). I was describing things lying in glass topped cases, with the cases up on legs and stands, all arranged around the room for easy access, when I noticed that someone at the target site was looking straight at me, as though she could see me. It startled me and for probably

---

[1] INSCOM is the abbreviation for the Army's Intelligence and Security Command.
[2] Stray Cat is a viewer acronym describing the Subconscious Transfer of Recollections, Anxieties, and Yearnings to Consciously Accessible Thought.

Evidential Details

the only time ever, I wasn't startled <u>out</u> of the session, but deeper into it. I looked back at her, and realized that it was the same girl who had been following the director and Joe in my earlier "dream", back in Augsburg. I looked directly at her, and started to say hello, but then she realized that I could see her, too, and she half turned, and disappeared. That threw me out of the session.

Fortunately, [Captain] Paul Smith was my monitor, and ever the curious one, when I told him what had happened, he said, "Let's follow her and see where she went." Through a series of very impromptu movement commands, we finally located her back at the place where she worked ... the Chinese psychic intelligence effort.

She appeared in some of my sessions after that, but rarely. I tried to find her several times, and a few of them succeeded. Apparently, what they defined as "session" and what we defined as "session" weren't the same. Anyway, over time, we struck up somewhat of a stand-offish acquaintance. About a year after that, I hadn't bumped into her again, so I did a session specifically to find her. She was then in college in a very large city, and evidently out of the government's project altogether. When I found her, she acknowledged my presence, and very strongly desired that we not have further contact. I backed out of the session, and haven't tried again, since. Don't cha love war stories?" [3]

Oct. 1, 1998 e-mail from Leonard Buchanan – Former Operational Database Manager 902nd Military Intelligence Unit - Fort Meade, Maryland and Owner of Problems> Solutions>Innovations, Inc.

You can actually access that person mentally and bring back their most deep-seated thoughts, feelings, emotions, motivations, fears, desires, drives, reservations, and everything else that might be there to drive their actions. It is, perhaps, in this one area where CRV [Controlled Remote Viewing] surpasses any other intelligence tool and finds its highest value.

Operation Star Gate's Data Base Manager
Leonard Buchanan in his book *The Seventh Sense*

---

[3] For more information, see, *China's Super Psychics* by Paul Dong and Thomas Raffill; Marlowe & Co. New York, 1997

Evidential Details

Remote Viewing Data Protocols

Surrounding the military's RV session protocols are the Operational Flow Protocols. The tasking agency was the "Customer" whose identity was strictly withheld to avoid inferences leading to Analytic Overlay. First published here, this process was classified for over two decades.

* * *

"In actual fact, there was pretty much a different work set-up every time we changed directors in the military unit which was pretty often as projects go. As a result, the "ideal plan" was never adhered to. Many times, we had to sort of switch horse in mid-stream. Anyway, here is the "ideal" workflow:

The **CUSTOMER** (Governmental Agency) comes to the unit director with a tasking.
The **UNIT DIRECTOR** meets with the customer and:
1) makes absolutely certain that the customer knows what CRV is and isn't – what it will and won't do.
2) looks the customer's problem over to see that it is the type of work we are best suited for. If not, he suggests a different solution for them.
If so, he then:
3) gets rid of the customer's "test" questions which only take up time and effort and accomplish nothing.
4) gets rid of the unnecessary questions – just fluff questions which the customer would like to have answered.
5) makes certain the questions asked are questions the customer really wants the answers to. There are LOTS of times when the customer will ask, "Who killed the victim", when the information he really wants is, "Where can we find the evidence that will show who killed the victim?"
6) agrees in writing on a set of basic questions which will be answered, once all the fluff and confusion is gotten out of the way.
7) makes certain that the Customer knows that these questions will be answered, and that other information will be provided, if it is found. However, if it isn't found, then the viewers are only responsible for what is being tasked. Follow-on questions will have to be asked later.
8) explains to the Customer the need for accurate feedback.
9) gets a definite commitment from the Customer that such feedback will be given, on each and every viewer's answer(s) to each and every question.
10) sets a commitment date for providing the answers. This must be a realistic date. Every Customer wants answers right now or yesterday, but

Evidential Details

the unit director needs to impress on the Customer that there are other customers who also have time limits of now or yesterday, and that reality must figure into the planning, like it or not.
11) provides the final list of questions to the Project Officer, along with any background information about the case gained from the customer.

The **PROJECT OFFICER** studies the background information and tasked questions and:
1) determines the main subject matter for each question.
2) decides the project number and fills out all the preliminary paperwork required for starting a new project.
3) provides the list of subjects to the Data Base Manager. The Data Base Manager looks up each information category in the data base and provides the Project Manager with a separate list of Viewers' names as suggested Viewers for each question.
4) determines which Viewers and Monitors should work on each question.
5) looks at the Viewers' and Monitors' existing schedules and determines the project's time line. He may even do a Pert chart to make scheduling easier.
6) "translates" each question into neutral wording.
7) notifies each Monitor and Viewer of the work schedule change.
8) generates an official tasking sheet to hand to each Monitor.

The **MONITOR** receives the tasking and coordinates from the Project Officer, along with any background information the Project Officer thinks the Monitor should know to help the Viewer better perform a productive session. The Monitor then:
1) makes certain he knows the Viewer's likes and dislikes, quirks, micro-movements, etc. If not, these are either looked up or found out from another Monitor who is more familiar with the Viewer.
2) gets information from the Database Manager about the Viewer's strengths and weaknesses. While this carries the danger of a "self-fulfilling prophecy", the Monitor is hopefully trained enough to use the information for formatting the session, rather than for guiding and leading the Viewer. If the Monitor is not this well trained, this step is passed up.
3) prepares the session workplace.
4) goes through the session with the Viewer.
5) helps the Viewer write the summary, if necessary.
6) after the paperwork is all done, provides both the Viewer's transcript and his (the Monitor's) session notes to the Analyst.

The **ANALYST** receives the paperwork and:
1) familiarizes himself with all the background knowledge.
2) collects the papers from all Viewer/Monitor pairs.
3) looks into his own notes on each and every Viewer to see work profiles

Evidential Details

(prone to using imagery, prone to using allegories, etc.). The Database Manager can be of help in this step.
4) performs analysis on the session (see the Analyst's Manual).
5) writes up his reports, critiques, summaries, etc. and provides it to the Report Writer.

The **REPORT WRITER** receives all the information from the Analyst and:
1) familiarizes himself with all the available background information.
2) familiarizes himself with all the Analyst's finding, interpretations and comments.
3) writes the final report (see the Report Writer's Manual)
NOTE!!! This includes taking the finalized answer to each Viewer to make certain that what is being reported is what the Viewer actually meant to say.
4) provides the final report to the Project Officer.

The **PROJECT OFFICER** then:
1) receives the finalized answers to each question after the session has been performed, analyzed and prepared for reporting.
2) gives final approval on the final report.
3) passes the final report to the Unit Director for delivery to the Customer.

The **UNIT DIRECTOR** then:
1) contacts the Customer and sets a date and time to go over the report. Information is not given ad hoc over the phone, nor is an "executive summary" provided.
2) meets with the Customer to provide the report.
3) once again makes certain that the Customer understands the CRV process, strengths and limitations.
4) explains what happened, and how each answer was obtained.
5) points out to the Customer that each question has a "dependability rating" beside it which will tell the Customer what each Viewer's track record is on each specific answer to each type of question. He explains how this "dependability rating" can be used by the Customer as an aid to making decisions from the information provided.
6) sets – in writing – a hard and definite "drop dead" date for feedback.
7) if/when feedback comes in, provides it to the Project Officer who handled the case.
8) if feedback doesn't come in, or is received incorrectly, it is returned to the Customer to either, "dun him" for feedback, or to re-explain how feed-back needs to be provided, formatted, etc.

The **PROJECT OFFICER** then:
1) evaluates each Viewer's response to each question against the feedback.
2) provides an evaluation to each Viewer.

Evidential Details

3) provides accurate data to the Database Manager for input into the database.
4) completes all summary paperwork for the project.
5) organizes all related paperwork, checks it for completeness, and prepares it for final storage and filing.

The **DATABASE MANAGER**:
1) inputs all received information into the database.
2) "massages" the database to provide information to those who need it. This includes the Training Officer and all Trainers.
3) maintains quality control on the data going in. "Garbage in – garbage out".

The **TRAINING OFFICER**:
1) schedules training times and facilities.
2) keeps evaluation reports on the Trainers.

The **TRAINER**:
1) accompanies new Viewers through the training process, analyzing their needs and progress every step of the way (see Trainers Manual).
2) makes and keeps records of the Viewer Student's "natural micro-movements". These will be provided to the Monitors along with a Viewer Student's profile of strengths and weakness.
3) advises management of the Viewer Student's progress and advises as to the student's best possible "training track" for providing the most useful and productive Viewer possible.

Needless to say, this is an overview, and not a complete list of responsibilities and obligations. For example, it doesn't cover what goes on in follow-on tasking, etc.

July 23, 1998 e-mail from: Leonard Buchanan– Former Operational Database Manager at the 902nd Military Intelligence Unit - Fort Meade, Maryland and Owner of Problems> Solutions>Innovations, Inc.

"The 'giggle factor' associated with remote viewing or psychic functioning continues to block earnest attempts at using these functions for humankind's benefit." - Joseph McMoneagle

Evidential Details

Beginnings

This details the basis for the original program funding. For readers interested in the data that justified more Congressional spending, this secretive overview of U.S. Military History is recommended.

CIA-Initiated Remote Viewing At Stanford Research Institute

by H. E. Puthoff, Ph.D.[25]
Institute for Advanced Studies at Austin
4030 Braker Lane W., #300
Austin, Texas 78759-5329

Abstract - In July 1995 the CIA declassified, and approved for release, documents revealing its sponsorship in the 1970s of a program at Stanford Research Institute in Menlo Park, CA, to determine whether such phenomena as remote viewing "might have any utility for intelligence collection" [1]. Thus began disclosure to the public of a two-decade-plus involvement of the intelligence community in the investigation of so-called para-psychological or psi phenomena. Presented here by the program's Founder and first Director (1972 - 1985) is the early history of the program, including discussion of some of the first, now declassified, results that drove early interest.

Introduction
On April 17, 1995, President Clinton issued Executive Order Nr. 1995-4-17, entitled Classified National Security Information. Although in one sense the order simply reaffirmed much of what has been long-standing policy, in another sense there was a clear shift toward more openness. In the opening

---

[25]Harold Puthoff received his BS and MS Degrees in Electrical Engineering at the University of Florida and a PhD from Stanford University in 1967. He went on to work at the National Security Agency at Fort Meade, Maryland as an Army engineer studying, lasers, high-speed computers, and fiber optics. He is the inventor of the tunable infra-red laser. He spent three years as a naval officer and worked eight years in the Microwave Laboratory at Stanford. Puthoff has over 31 technical papers published on such topics as electron-beam devices, lasers and quantum zero-point-energy effects. He reportedly has patents issued in the areas of energy fields, laser, and communications. [author]

paragraph, for example, we read: "In recent years, however, dramatic changes have altered, although not eliminated, the national security threats that we confront. These changes provide a greater opportunity to emphasize our commitment to open Government." In the Classification Standards section of the Order this commitment is operationalized by phrases such as "If there is significant doubt about the need to classify information, it shall not be classified." Later in the document, in reference to information that requires continued protection, there even appears the remarkable phrase "In some exceptional cases, however, the need to protect such information may be outweighed by the public interest in disclosure of the information, and in these cases the information should be declassified."

A major fallout of this reframing of attitude toward classification is that there is enormous pressure on those charged with maintaining security to work hard at being responsive to reasonable requests for disclosure. One of the results is that FOIA (Freedom of Information Act) requests that have languished for months to years are suddenly being acted upon.[1]

One outcome of this change in policy is the government's recent admission of its two-decade-plus involvement in funding highly-classified, special access programs in remote viewing (RV) and related psi phenomena, first at Stanford Research Institute (SRI) and then at Science Applications International Corporation (SAIC), both in Menlo Park, CA, supplemented by various in-house government programs. Although almost all of the documentation remains yet classified, in July 1995 270 pages of SRI reports were declassified and released by the CIA, the program's first sponsor [2]. Thus, although through the years columns by Jack Anderson and others had claimed leaks of "psychic spy" programs with such exotic names as Grill Flame, Center Lane, Sunstreak and Star Gate, CIA's release of the SRI reports constitutes the first documented public admission of significant intelligence community involvement in the psi area.

As a consequence of the above, although I had founded the program in early 1972, and had acted as its Director until I left in 1985 to head up the Institute for Advanced Studies at Austin (at which point my colleague Ed May assumed responsibility as Director), it was not until 1995 that I found myself for the first time able to utter in a single sentence the connected acronyms CIA/SRI/RV. In this report I discuss the genesis of the program, report on some of the early, now declassified, results that drove early interest, and outline the general direction the program took as it expanded into a multi-year, multi-site, multi-million-dollar effort to determine whether such phenomena as remote viewing "might have any utility for intelligence collection" [1].

Beginnings

Evidential Details

In early 1972, I was involved in laser research at Stanford Research Institute (now called SRI International) in Menlo Park, CA. At that time I was also circulating a proposal to obtain a small grant for some research in quantum biology. In that proposal I had raised the issue whether physical theory as we knew it was capable of describing life processes, and had suggested some measurements involving plants and lower organisms [3]. This proposal was widely circulated, and a copy was sent to Cleve Backster in New York City who was involved in measuring the electrical activity of plants with standard polygraph equipment. New York artist Ingo Swann chanced to see my proposal during a visit to Backster's lab, and wrote me suggesting that if I were interested in investigating the boundary between the physics of the animate and inanimate, I should consider experiments of the parapsychological type. Swann then went on to describe some apparently successful experiments in psychokinesis in which he had participated at Prof. Gertrude Schmeidler's laboratory at the City College of New York. As a result of this correspondence I invited him to visit SRI for a week in June 1972 to demonstrate such effects, frankly, as much out of personal scientific curiosity as anything else.

Prior to Swann's visit I arranged for access to a well-shielded magneto-meter used in a quark-detection experiment in the Physics Department at Stanford University. During our visit to this laboratory, sprung as a surprise to Swann, he appeared to perturb the operation of the magnetometer, located in a vault below the floor of the building and shielded by mu-metal shielding, an aluminum container, copper shielding and a superconducting shield. As if to add insult to injury, he then went on to "remote view" the interior of the apparatus, rendering by drawing a reasonable facsimile of its rather complex (and heretofore unpublished) construction. It was this latter feat that impressed me perhaps even more than the former, as it also eventually did representatives of the intelligence community. I wrote up these observations and circulated it among my scientific colleagues in draft form of what was eventually published as part of a conference proceeding [4].

In a few short weeks a pair of visitors showed up at SRI with the above report in hand. Their credentials showed them to be from the CIA. They knew of my previous background as a Naval Intelligence Officer and then civilian employee at the National Security Agency (NSA) several years earlier, and felt they could discuss their concerns with me openly. There was, they told me, increasing concern in the intelligence community about the level of effort in Soviet parapsychology being funded by the Soviet security services [5]; by Western scientific standards the field was considered nonsense by most working scientists. As a result they had been on the

Evidential Details

lookout for a research laboratory outside of academia that could handle a quiet, low-profile classified investigation, and SRI appeared to fit the bill. They asked if I could arrange an opportunity for them to carry out some simple experiments with Swann, and, if the tests proved satisfactory, would I consider a pilot program along these lines? I agreed to consider this, and arranged for the requested tests. [2]

The tests were simple, the visitors simply hiding objects in a box and asking Swann to attempt to describe the contents. The results generated in these experiments are perhaps captured most eloquently by the following example. In one test Swann said "I see something small, brown and irregular, sort of like a leaf or something that resembles it, except that it seems very much alive, like it's even moving!" The target chosen by one of the visitors turned out to be a small live moth, which indeed did look like a leaf. Although not all responses were quite so precise, nonetheless the integrated results were sufficiently impressive that in short order an eight-month, $49,909 Biofield Measurements Program was negotiated as a pilot study, a laser colleague Russell Targ who had had a long-time interest and involvement in parapsychology joined the program, and the experimental effort was begun in earnest.

Early Remote Viewing Results

During the eight-month pilot study of remote viewing the effort gradually evolved from the remote viewing of symbols and objects in envelopes and boxes, to the remote viewing of local target sites in the San Francisco Bay area, demarked by outbound experimenters sent to the site under strict protocols devised to prevent artifactual results. Later judging of the results were similarly handled by double-blind protocols designed to foil artifactual matching. Since these results have been presented in detail elsewhere, both in the scientific literature [6-8] and in popular book format [9], I direct the interested reader to these sources. To summarize, over the years the back-and-forth criticism of protocols, refinement of methods, and successful replication of this type of remote viewing in independent laboratories [10-14], has yielded considerable scientific evidence for the reality of the phenomenon. Adding to the strength of these results was the discovery that a growing number of individuals could be found to demonstrate high-quality remote viewing, often to their own surprise, such as the talented Hella Hammid. As a separate issue, however, most convincing to our early program monitors were the results now to be described, generated under their own control.

First, during the collection of data for a formal remote viewing series targeting indoor laboratory apparatus and outdoor locations (a series

Evidential Details

eventually published in toto in the Proc. IEEE [7]), the CIA contract monitors, ever watchful for possible chicanery, participated as remote viewers themselves in order to critique the protocols. In this role three separate viewers, designated visitors V1 - V3 in the IEEE paper, contributed seven of the 55 viewings, several of striking quality. Reference to the IEEE paper for a comparison of descriptions/ drawings to pictures of the associated targets, generated by the contract monitors in their own viewings, leaves little doubt as to why the contract monitors came to the conclusion that there was something to remote viewing (see, for example, Figure 1 herein).

Figure 1 - Sketches of Target

Figure 2 – Target merry-go-round

As summarized in the Executive Summary of the now-released Final Report [2] of the second year of the program, "The development of this capability at SRI has evolved to the point where visiting CIA personnel with no previous exposure to such concepts have performed well under controlled laboratory conditions (that is, generated target descriptions of sufficiently high quality to permit blind matching of descriptions to targets by independent judges)." What happened next, however, made even these results pale in comparison.

Coordinate Remote Viewing

To determine whether it was necessary to have a "beacon" individual at the target site, Swann suggested carrying out an experiment to remote view the planet Jupiter before the upcoming NASA Pioneer 10 fly by. In that case, much to his chagrin (and ours) he found a ring around Jupiter, and wondered if perhaps he had remote viewed Saturn by mistake. Our colleagues in astronomy were quite unimpressed as well, until the flyby revealed that an unanticipated ring did in fact exist. [3] Expanding the protocols yet further, Swann proposed a series of experiments in which the target was designated not by sending a "beacon" person to the target site, but rather by the use of geographical coordinates, latitude and longitude in degrees, minutes and seconds. Needless to say, this proposal seemed even more outrageous than "ordinary" remote viewing. The difficulties in taking this proposal seriously, designing protocols to eliminate the possibility of a combination of globe memorization and eidetic or photographic memory, and so forth, are discussed in considerable detail in Reference [9]. Suffice it to say that investigation of this approach, which we designated Scanate (scanning by coordinate), eventually provided us with sufficient evidence to bring it up to the contract monitors and suggest a test under their control. A description of that test and its results, carried out in mid-1973 during the initial pilot study, are best presented by quoting directly from the Executive Summary of the Final Report of the second year's follow-up program [2]. The remote viewers were Ingo Swann and Pat Price, and the entire transcripts are available in the released documents [2].

In order to subject the remote viewing phenomena to a rigorous long distance test under external control, a request for geographical coordinates of a site unknown to subject and experimenters was forwarded to the OSI group responsible for threat analysis in this area. In response, SRI personnel received a set of geographical coordinates (latitude and longitude in degrees, minutes, and seconds) of a facility, hereafter referred to as the West Virginia Site. The experimenters then carried out a remote viewing experiment on a double-blind basis, that is, blind to experimenters as well as subject. The experiment had as its goal the determination of the utility of remote viewing under conditions approximating an operational scenario. Two subjects targeted on the site, a sensitive installation. One subject drew a detailed map of the building and grounds layout, the other provided information about the interior including code words, data subsequently verified by sponsor sources (report available from COTR).[4]

Since details concerning the site's mission in general, [5] and evaluation of the remote viewing test in particular, remain highly classified to this day, all that can be said is that interest in the client community was heightened considerably following this exercise.

Because Price found the above exercise so interesting, as a personal challenge he went on to scan the other side of the globe for a

Communist Bloc equivalent and found one located in the Urals, the detailed description of which is also included in Ref. [2]. As with the West Virginia Site, the report for the Urals Site was also verified by personnel in the sponsor organization as being substantially correct.

What makes the West Virginia/Urals Sites viewings so remarkable is that these are not best-ever examples culled out of a longer list; these are literally the first two site-viewings carried out in a simulated operational-type scenario. In fact, for Price these were the very first two remote viewings in our program altogether, and he was invited to participate in yet further experimentation.

Operational Remote Viewing (Semipalatinsk, USSR)

Midway through the second year of the program (July 1974) our CIA sponsor decided to challenge us to provide data on a Soviet site of ongoing operational significance. Pat Price was the remote viewer. A description of the remote viewing, taken from our declassified final report [2], reads as given below. I cite this level of detail to indicate the thought that goes into such an "experiment" to minimize cueing while at the same time being responsive to the requirements of an operational situation. Again, this is not a "best-ever" example from a series of such viewings, but rather the very first operational Soviet target concerning which we were officially tasked. "To determine the utility of remote viewing under operational conditions, a long-distance remote viewing experiment was carried out on a sponsor designated target of current interest, an unidentified research center at Semipalatinsk, USSR.

This experiment, carried out in three phases, was under direct control of the COTR. To begin the experiment, the COTR furnished map coordinates in degrees, minutes and seconds. The only additional information provided was the designation of the target as an R&D test facility. The experimenters then closeted themselves with Subject S1, gave him the map coordinates and indicated the designation of the target as an R&D test facility. A remote-viewing experiment was then carried out. This activity constituted Phase I of the experiment.

Figure 3 shows the subject's graphic effort for building layout; Figure 4 shows the subject's particular attention to a multistory gantry crane he observed at the site. Both results were obtained by the experimenters on a double-blind basis before exposure to any additional COTR-held information, thus eliminating the possibility of cueing. These results were turned over to the client representatives for evaluation. For comparison, an artist's rendering of the site as known to the COTR (but not to the experimenters until later) is shown in Figure 5.

Evidential Details

Were the results not promising, the experiment would have stopped at this point. Description of the multistory crane, however, a relatively unusual target item, was taken as indicative of possible target acquisition. Therefore, Phase II was begun, defined by the subject being made "witting" (of the client) by client representatives who introduced themselves to the subject at that point; Phase II also included a second round of experimentation on the Semipalatinsk site with direct participation of client representatives in which further data were obtained and evaluated. As preparation for this phase, client representatives purposely kept themselves blind to all but general knowledge of the target site to minimize the possibility of cueing. The Phase II effort was focused on the generation of physical data that could be independently verified by other client sources, thus providing a calibration of the process.

The end of Phase II gradually evolved into the first part of Phase III, the generation of unverifiable data concerning the Semipalatinsk site not available to the client, but of operational interest nonetheless. Several hours of tape transcript and a notebook of drawings were generated over a two-week period.

Figure 3 - Subject effort at building layout

Figure 4 - Subject effort construction crane

The data describing the Semipalatinsk site were evaluated by the sponsor, and are contained in a separate report. In general, several details concerning the salient technology of the Semipalatinsk site appeared to dovetail with data from other sources, and a number of specific large structural elements were correctly described. The results contained noise along with the signal, but were nonetheless clearly differentiated from the chance results that were generated by control subjects in comparison experiments carried out by the COTR."

For discussion of the ambiance and personal factors involved in carrying out this experiment, along with further detail generated as Price (see Figure 6) "roamed" the facility, including detailed comparison of Price's RV-generated information with later determined "ground-truth reality," see the accompanying article by Russell Targ in the Journal of Scientific Exploration <http:// www. jse.com/>, Vol. 10, No. 1.

Additional experiments having implications for intelligence concerns were carried out, such as the remote viewing of cipher machine type apparatus, and the RV-sorting of sealed envelopes to differentiate those that contained letters with secret writing from those that did not. To discuss these here in detail would take us too far afield, but the interested reader can follow up by referring to the now-declassified project documents [2].

Figure 5 - Actual COTR rendering of Semipalatinsk, USSR target site.

Follow-on Programs

The above discussion brings us up to the end of 1975. As a result of the material being generated by both SRI and CIA remote viewers, interest in the program in government circles, especially within the intelligence community, intensified considerably and led to an ever increasing briefing schedule. This in turn led to an ever-increasing number of clients, contracts and tasking, and therefore expansion of the program to a multi-client base, and eventually to an integrated joint-services program under single-agency (DIA)[6] leadership. To meet the demand for the increased level of effort we first increased our professional staff by inviting Ed May to join the program in 1976, then screened and added to the program a cadre of remote viewers as consultants, and let subcontracts to increase our scope of activity.

As the program expanded, in only a very few cases could the client's identities and program tasking be revealed. Examples include a NASA-funded study negotiated early in the program by Russ Targ to determine whether the internal state of an electronic random-number-generator could

Evidential Details

be detected by RV processes [16], and a study funded by the Naval Electronics Systems Command to determine whether attempted remote viewing of distant light flashes would induce correlated changes in the viewer's brainwave (EEG) production [17]. For essentially all other projects, during my 14-yr. tenure at SRI, however, the identity of the clients and most of the tasking were classified and remain so today. (The exception was the occasional privately funded study.) We are told, however, that further declassification and release of much of this material is almost certain to occur.

What can be said, then, about further development of the program in the two decades following 1975?[7] In broad terms it can be said that much of the SRI effort was directed not so much toward developing an operational U.S. capability, but rather toward assessing the threat potential of its use against the U.S. by others.

The words 'threat assessment' were often used to describe the program's purpose during its development, especially during the early years. As a result much of the remote-viewing activity was carried out under conditions where ground-truth reality was a priori known or could be determined, such as the description of U.S. facilities and technological developments, the timing of rocket test firings and underground nuclear tests, and the location of individuals and mobile units. And, of course, we were responsive to requests to provide assistance during such events as the loss of an airplane or the taking of hostages, relying on the talents of an increasing cadre of remote-viewer/ consultants, some well-known in the field such as Keith Harary, and many who have not surfaced publicly until recently, such as Joe McMoneagle.

One might ask whether in this program RV-generated information was ever of sufficient significance as to influence decisions at a policy level. This is of course impossible to determine unless policymakers were to come forward with a statement in the affirmative. One example of a possible candidate is a study we performed at SRI during the Carter administration debates concerning proposed deployment of the mobile MX missile system.

In that scenario missiles were to be randomly shuffled from silo to silo in a silo field, in a form of high-tech shell game. In a computer simulation of a twenty-silo field with randomly-assigned (hidden) missile locations, we were able, using RV-generated data, to show rather forcefully that the application of a sophisticated statistical averaging technique (sequential sampling) could in principle permit an adversary to defeat the system. I briefed these results to the appropriate offices at their request, and a written report with the technical details was widely circulated among groups responsible for threat analysis [18], and with some impact. What role, if any, our small contribution played in the mix of factors behind the enormously complex decision to cancel the program will probably never be known, and must of course a priori be considered in all likelihood negligible. Nonetheless, this is a prototypical example of the kind of tasking that by its nature potentially had policy implications.

Figure 6 - Left to right: Christopher Green,[26] Pat Price,[27] and Hal Puthoff. Picture taken following a successful experiment involving glider-ground RV.

Even though the details of the broad range of experiments, some brilliant successes, many total failures, have not yet been released, we have nonetheless been able to publish summaries of what was learned in these studies about the overall characteristics of remote viewing, as in Table 5 of Reference [8]. Furthermore, over the years we were able to address certain questions of scientific interest in a rigorous way and to publish the results in the open literature. Examples include the apparent lack of attenuation of remote viewing due to seawater shielding (submersible experiments) [8], the amplification of RV performance by use of error-correcting coding techniques [19, 20], and the utility of a technique we call associational remote viewing (ARV) to generate useful predictive information [21].8

---

[26] Dr. Christopher Green MD. Neurophysiology, received the CIA's National Intelligence Medal as a Scientific Advisory Board Member to the CIA's Directorate of Intelligence.
[27] One of the finest remote viewers ever, Pat Price, a former police commissioner and councilman in Burbank, CA, came to the Government's attention when he viewed officers, interiors, and files at the virtually unknown, nuclear hardened Naval Satellite Intelligence site in West Virginia. When the Pentagon was shown the data, Price was interrogated by the U.S. Defense Investigative Service who demanded to know who had breached security and how they did it. He is reputed to be the only viewer that could read numbers and letters on a target. Later he viewed inside the Soviet installation at Mount Narodnaya in the Ural Mountains. He went on to work for the CIA and is reputed to have died of a heart attack in July of 1975, in Las Vegas. Even though he was supposedly dead on arrival at the hospital, no autopsy was performed. Suspicions have always existed about the truth of his death. [author]

Evidential Details

As a sociological aside, we note that the overall efficacy of remote viewing in a program like this was not just a scientific issue. For example, when the Semipalatinsk data described earlier was forwarded for analysis, one group declined to get involved because the whole concept was unscientific nonsense, while a second group declined because, even though it might be real, it was possibly demonic; a third group had to be found. And, as in the case of public debate about such phenomena, the program's image was on occasion as likely to be damaged by an over enthusiastic supporter, as by a detractor. Personalities, politics and personal biases were always factors to be dealt with.

Official Statements/Perspectives

With regard to admission by the government of its use of remote viewers under operational conditions, officials have on occasion been relatively forthcoming. President Carter, in a speech to college students in Atlanta in September 1995, is quoted by Reuters as saying that during his administration a plane went down in Zaire, and a meticulous sweep of the African terrain by American spy satellites failed to locate any sign of the wreckage. It was then "without my knowledge" that the head of the CIA (Adm. Stansfield Turner) turned to a woman reputed to have psychic powers. As told by Carter, "she gave some latitude and longitude figures. We focused our satellite cameras on that point and the plane was there." Independently, Turner himself also has admitted the Agency's use of a remote viewer (in this case, Pat Price).[9] And recently, in a segment taped for the British television series Equinox [22], Maj. Gen. Ed Thompson, Assistant Chief of Staff for Intelligence, U.S. Army (1977-1981), volunteered "I had one or more briefings by SRI and was impressed.... The decision I made was to set up a small, in-house, low-cost effort in remote viewing...."

Finally, a recent unclassified report [23] prepared for the CIA by the American Institutes for Research (AIR), concerning a remote viewing effort carried out under a DIA program called Star Gate (discussed in detail elsewhere in this volume), cites the roles of the CIA and DIA in the history of the program, including acknowledgment that a cadre of full-time government employees used remote viewing techniques to respond to tasking from operational military organizations. [10]

As information concerning the various programs spawned by intelligence-community interest is released, and the dialog concerning their scientific and social significance is joined, the results are certain to be hotly debated. Bearing witness to this fact are the companion articles in this volume by Ed May, Director of the SRI and SAIC programs since 1985, and by Jessica Utts and Ray Hyman, consultants on the AIR evaluation cited

Evidential Details

above. These articles address in part the AIR study. That study, limited in scope to a small fragment of the overall program effort, resulted in a conclusion that although laboratory research showed statistically significant results, use of remote viewing in intelligence gathering was not warranted.

Regardless of one's a priori position, however, an unimpassioned observer cannot help but attest to the following fact. Despite the ambiguities inherent in the type of exploration covered in these programs, the integrated results appear to provide unequivocal evidence of a human capacity to access events remote in space and time, however falteringly, by some cognitive process not yet understood. My years of involvement as a research manager in these programs have left me with the conviction that this fact must be taken into account in any attempt to develop an unbiased picture of the structure of reality.

Footnotes

1 - One example being the release of documents that are the subject of this report - see the memoir by Russell Targ.

2 - Since the reputation of the intelligence services is mixed among members of the general populace, I have on occasion been challenged as to why I would agree to cooperate with the CIA or other elements of the intelligence community in this work. My answer is simply that as a result of my own previous exposure to this community I became persuaded that war can almost always be traced to a failure in intelligence, and that therefore the strongest weapon for peace is good intelligence.

3 - This result was published by us in advance of the ring's discovery [9].

4 - Editor's footnote added here: COTR - Contracting Officer's Technical Representative.

5 - An NSA listening post at the Navy's Sugar Grove facility, according to intelligence-community chronicler Bamford [15]

6 - DIA - Defense Intelligence Agency. The CIA dropped out as a major player in the mid-seventies due to pressure on the Agency (unrelated to the RV Program) from the Church-Pike Congressional Committee.

7 - See also the contribution by Ed May elsewhere in this volume concerning his experiences from 1985 on during his tenure as Director.

8 - For example, one application of this technique yielded not only a published, statistically significant result, but also a return of $26,000 in 30 days in the silver futures market [21].

9 - The direct quote is given in Targ's contribution elsewhere in this volume.

10 - "From 1986 to the first quarter of FY 1995, the DoD para-normal psychology program received more than 200 tasks from operational military organizations requesting that the program staff apply a paranormal psychological technique know (sic) as "remote viewing" (RV) to attain information unavailable from other sources." [23]

References

[1] "*CIA Statement on 'Remote Viewing*," CIA Public Affairs Office, 6 September 1995.

[2] Harold E. Puthoff and Russell Targ, "*Perceptual Augmentation Techniques,*" SRI Progress Report No. 3 (31 Oct. 1974) and Final Report (1 Dec. 1975) to the CIA, covering the period January 1974 through February 1975, the second year of the program. This effort was funded at the level of $149,555.

[3] H. E. Puthoff, "*Toward a Quantum Theory of Life Process,*" unpubl proposal, Stanford Research Institute (1972).

[4] H. E. Puthoff and R. Targ, "*Physics, Entropy and Psycho-kinesis,*" in Proc. Conf. Quantum

Evidential Details

Physics and Parapsychology (Geneva, Switzerland); (New York: Parapsychology Foundation, 1975).

[5] Documented in "*Paraphysics R&D - Warsaw Pact* (U)," DST-1810S-202-78, Defense Intelligence Agency (30 March 1978).

[6] R. Targ and H. E. Puthoff, "*Information Transfer under Conditions of Sensory Shielding,*" Nature 252, 602 (1974).

[7] H. E. Puthoff and R. Targ, "*A Perceptual Channel for Information Transfer over Kilometer Distances: Historical Perspective and Recent Research,*" Proc. IEEE 64, 329 (1976).

[8] H. E. Puthoff, R. Targ and E. C. May, "*Experimental Psi Research: Implications for Physics,*" in The Role of Consciousness in the Physical World", edited by R. G. Jahn (AAAS Selected Symposium 57, Westview Press, Boulder, 1981).

[9] R. Targ and H. E. Puthoff, *Mind Reach* (Delacorte Press, New York, 1977).

[10] J. P. Bisaha and B. J. Dunne, "*Multiple Subject and Long-Distance Precognitive Remote Viewing of Geographical Locations,*" in Mind at Large, edited by C. T. Tart, H. E. Puthoff and R. Targ (Praeger, New York, 1979), p. 107.

[11] B. J. Dunne and J. P. Bisaha, "*Precognitive Remote Viewing in the Chicago Area: a Replication of the Stanford Experiment,*" J. Parapsychology 43, 17 (1979).

[12] R. G. Jahn, "*The Persistent Paradox of Psychic Phenomena: An Engineering Perspective,*" Proc. IEEE 70, 136 (1982).

[13] R. G. Jahn and B. J. Dunne, "*On the Quantum Mechanics of Consciousness with Application to Anomalous Phenomena,*" Found. Phys. 16, 721 (1986).

[14] R. G. Jahn and B. J. Dunne, *Margins of Reality* (Harcourt, Brace and Jovanovich, New York, 1987).

[15] J. Bamford, *The Puzzle Palace* (Penguin Books, New York, 1983) pp. 218-222.

[16] R. Targ, P. Cole and H. E. Puthoff, "*Techniques to Enhance Man/Machine Communication,*" Stanford Research Institute Final Report on NASA Project NAS7-100 (August 1974).

[17] R. Targ, E. C. May, H. E. Puthoff, D. Galin and R. Ornstein, "*Sensing of Remote EM Sources* (Physiological Correlates)," SRI Intern'l Final Report on Naval Electronics Systems Command Project N00039-76-C-0077, covering the period November 1975 - to October 1976 (April 1978).

[18] H. E. Puthoff, "*Feasibility Study on the Vulnerability of the MPS System to RV Detection Techniques,*" SRI Internal Report, 15 April 1979; revised 2 May 1979.

[19] H. E. Puthoff, "*Calculator-Assisted Psi Amplification,*" Research in Parapsychology 1984, edited by Rhea White and J. Solfvin (Scarecrow Press, Metuchen, NJ, 1985), p. 48.

[20] H. E. Puthoff, "*Calculator-Assisted Psi Amplification II: Use of the Sequential-Sampling Technique as a Variable-Length Majority-Vote Code,*" Research in Parapsychology 1985, edited by D. Weiner and D. Radin (Scarecrow Press, Metuchen, NJ, 1986), p. 73.

[21] H. E. Puthoff, "*ARV (Associational Remote Viewing) Applications,*" Research in Parapsychology 1984, edited by Rhea White and J. Solfvin (Scarecrow Press, Metuchen, NJ, 1985), p. 121.

[22] "*The Real X-Files*", Independent Channel 4, England (shown 27 August 1995); to be shown in the U.S. on the Discovery Channel.

[23] M. D. Mumford, A. M. Rose and D. Goslin, "*An Evaluation of Remote Viewing: Research and Applications*", American Institutes for Research (September 29, 1995).

Copyright 1996 by Dr. H.E. Puthoff.
Permission to redistribute granted, but only in complete and unaltered form.

[Footnotes are designed to facilitate a greater understanding of Remote Viewing pioneers, but are not original. None of Dr. Puthoff's text was altered.]

Evidential Details

Targeted Reading

Because of its capabilities Remote Viewing disinformation exists which discourages further interest. This list was assembled to help people locate books directly from members of the program involved in this most fascinating component of United States Military History.

Books by Members of the U.S. Military Program

McMoneagle, Joseph W.

- *Mind Trek*; Hampton Roads, 1993
- *The Ultimate Time Machine*; Hampton Roads, 1998
- *Remote Viewing Secrets*; Hampton Roads, 2000
- *The Stargate Chronicles*; Hampton Roads, 2002
- *Memoirs of a Psychic Spy: The Remarkable Life of U. S. Government Remote Viewer 001*; Hampton Roads, 2006

Buchanan, Leonard

- *The Seventh Sense – The Secrets of Remote Viewing as Told by a "Psychic Spy" for the U.S. Military*; Paraview Pocket Books, 2003
- *Remote Viewing Methods - Remote Viewing and Remote Influencing*; DVD, 2004

Smith, Paul H.

- *Reading the Enemy's Mind - Inside Stargate - America's Psychic Espionage Program*; Tor non-fiction, 2005

Morehouse, David A.

- *Psychic Warrior – Inside the CIA's Stargate Program: The True Story of a Soldiers Espionage and Awakening*; St Martin's Press, 1996
- *Nonlethal Weapons: War Without Death*; Praeger Publishers, 1996
- *Remote Viewing: The Complete User's Manual for Coordinate Remote Viewing*; Sounds True Publishers, 2011

Puthoff, Harold E. with Russell Targ

- *Mind Reach - Scientists Look at Psychic Abilities*; Delacorte, 1977 & New World Library, 2004

Swann, Ingo

- *To Kiss the Earth Goodbye*; Hawthorne, New York, 1975

Evidential Details

- *Star Fire*, Dell non-fiction, 1978
- *Natural ESP: The ESP Core and its Raw Characteristics* with Harold E. Puthoff; Bantam Books, 1987
- *Everybody's Guide to Natural ESP: Unlocking the Extrasensory Power of Your Mind*; Jeremy P. Tharcher Imprint, 1991
- *Your Nostradamus Factor*; Fireside Press, 1993
- *Remote Viewing & ESP From The Inside Out*; DVD

Targ, Russell

- *Mind Race: Understanding and Using Psychic Abilities*, with Keith Harary; Ballantine Books, 1984
- Miracles of Mind: Exploring Nonlocal Consciousness and Spiritual Healing; New World Library, 1999
- Limitless Mind: A Guide to Remote Viewing and Transformation of Consciousness; New World Library, 2004
- *Do you See What I See?*; ESP and the C.I.A. and the Meaning of Life; Hampton Roads, 2010
- *The Reality of ESP: A Physicists Proof of Psychic Abilities*; Quest Books, 2012

Atwater, F. Holmes
- Captain of My Ship, Master of My Soul: Living with Guidance; Hampton Roads Publishing, 2001

Other Sources

Radin, Dean I.
- *The Conscious Universe: The Scientific Truth of Psychic Phenomena*; Harper Edge, 1997

- *Entangled Minds: Extrasensory Experiences in a Quantum Reality*, Paraview Pocket Books, 2006

- Moreno, Jonathon D. - *Mind Wars: Brain Science and the Military in the 21st Century*; Bellevue Literary Press, 2012

- Schnabel, Jim – *Remote Viewers: The Secret History of America's Psychic Spies*; Dell–non-fiction, 1997

- McRae, Ronald – *Mind Wars: The true story of Government Research into the Military Potential of Psychic Weapons*; St Martin's Press, 1984

Evidential Details

Other Series Books

Lae City Airport, New Guinea - July, 1937 – Get into the cockpit for the last flight of the vanished pilot **Amelia Earhart**. Learn of the plane's unknown final flight trajectory, cockpit circumstances and final thoughts in her last minute of life. Entered into four libraries within six months, including Purdue University's Earhart Special Collection Library, the book includes a "how to find the debris field" location map with yardages and points of reference including a flight scenario that has never been put forward. With the failures of the TIGHAR Group insiders have subsequently blogged that our scenario is the one worth investigating.

Ötzal Alps Mountains - Italian-Austrian border ~ 3,300 BC – Follow the trail of Europe's archeological "show of the century." Learn the whereabouts of **Ötzi the Iceman**'s unknown home camp and why and how he died alone in the mountains which some still regard as a Neolithic crime scene. This book includes remote viewing maps, pre-destruction tool drawings, including an undiscovered tool, his cabin, and the world's only real time portrait considered significant enough that the Museum in Bolzano, Italy obtained its copywrite release for Ötzi's 20th Anniversary exhibit. Interwoven with scientific quotation, this account also includes specifics of his tribal life in what we first identified as the Langtaufers Valley. The book provides Ötzi's previously unknown eight day course through the mountains using modern Alpine trail numbers. Learn the cause for his violent falling death which was first brought forward for peer review in this book.

Onboard RMS Titanic - North Atlantic - April, 1912 – In the first book to appear after the revelations of the 2nd Officer's granddaughter, review the Evidential Details substantiating the amazing crow's nest developments as *Titanic* bore down on the ice. Then, move to a resolution regarding **Captain E. J. Smith's** final actions before his previously unknown non-drowning death. The book includes obscure artifact drawings whose existence was only confirmed through ocean floor salvage efforts after our remote viewing sessions. Read history's only narrative of the last 20 minutes as the ship prepared to take over 1500 terrified passengers down into the frigid black ocean at 2:18 in the morning.

Execution Square - Rouen, France - May, 1431 – Go to the stake in the market square for the ghastly burning of the military heroine lost in the mists of time - **Joan of Arc**. Highlighted are her military successes, capture, and some trial excerpts. These sessions provide an amazingly detailed architectural description of Rouen city's medieval square exactly as Joan saw it. Learn of the prosecutor's motivations, and the fears of the spectators and the British soldiers. McMoneagle's renowned artwork documents the scene when she was chained to the burning scaffold and includes history's only portrait of this previously faceless Saint.

Streets of Whitechapel - London, England – Jack the Ripper - Fall, 1888 – A human energy comparison from suspect James Maybrick's death bed in Liverpool, England, to an actual Ripping in progress in Whitechapel. This book provides the world's only portraits of Jack and his victim (Elizabeth Stride) moments before her death. Get inside Jack's head and learn of his motivations. The book includes a draftsmen's drawing of his mysterious knife and exposes how this apprehended criminal remained a mystery because of his negotiated state secret status circumventing British Law. Then learn of his victim's statistically even more unusual behavior.

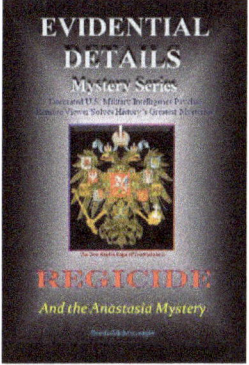

The Evidential Details fine line of *You Are There* mysteries solved.

Evidential Details

Princess Diana

[i] McMoneagle, Joseph W., *Remote Viewing Secrets – A Handbook*; Hampton Roads Publishing Company, Inc. 2000 p. xv
[ii] McMoneagle, Joseph W., *The Stargate Chronicles*; Hampton Roads Publishing Company, Inc. 2002 p. 182
[iii] Simmons, Simone, *Diana – The Secret Years* with Susan Hill; Ballantine Books 1998 p.120
[iv] Delorm, Rene, *Diana & Dodi - A Love Story - By the Butler Who Saw Their Romance Blossom*, with Barry Fox and Nadine Taylor; Tallfellow Press 1998 p.144
[v] Anderson, Christopher, *The Day Diana Died*; William Morrow and Company 1998 p.114
[vi] Anderson; p.113
[vii] Delorm; p.154
[viii] ibid; p.154
[ix] The Learning Channel Presentation - *Princess Diana*; A Fulcrum Production; a Granada Presentation for ITV 1998; hereafter referred to as *TLC*
[x] Delorm; p.155
[xi] Anderson; p.99
[xii] ibid; p.166
[xiii] Sancton, Thomas and Scott MacLeod, *Death of a Princess - The Investigation*; St. Martin's Press 1998 p.157
[xiv] Delorm; p.157
[xv] ibid; p.158
[xvi] Spoto, Donald, *Diana - The Last Year*;; Harmony Books 1997 p. 171
[xvii] Sanction; p.158-9
[xviii] TLC - Mohammed Al-Fayed interview
[xix] Junor, Penny, *Charles - Victim or Villain*; Harper Collins Publishers 1998; p.18
[xx] Sanction; p.167
[xxi] Final Report - Paris Prosecutor's Office; Head of the Prosecution Department at Courts of the First Instance; Examining Magistrates Hervé Stephan and Christine Devidal
[xxii] TLC - documentary information
[xxiii] TLC - interview with Dr. Martin Skinner.
[xxiv] Anderson; p.191
[xxv] Interview with Mohammed Al Fayed as per his internet site address:www.alfayed.com/indexie4.html, as published to the Internet on October 25, 1998
[xxvi] Spoto; p.172
[xxvii] Sanction; p 251
[xxviii] ibid; p. 6
[xxix] *Newsweek* Magazine; September 8, 1997; p. 33
[xxx] ibid; p. 241
[xxxi] Buchanan, Lyn, *The Seventh Sense*, Paraview Pocket Books, 2003, p. 190
[xxxii] Sanction; p. 17
[xxxiii] ibid; p.17 - 18
[xxxiv] Junor; p. 20
[xxxv] Spoto; p.180
[xxxvi] Junor; p. 22
[xxxvii] *French Final Accident Report* – Conclusionary Statement section
[xxxviii] Lyall, Sarah; New York Times; December 15, 2008

Civil War

[xxxix] Hill, Daniel Harvey, Lieutenant General, C.S.A., "The Battle of South Mountain, or Boonsboro"; *Battles And Leaders of the Civil War, Vol. II 1887*; p. 565, hereafter referred to as B&L
[xl] *The Official Records of the War of the Rebellion*, Vol. XIX, Part ii, pp. 590-603, hereafter

Evidential Details

[xli] referred to as OR
[xlii] Hood, J.B., Lt. Gen, CSA, *Advance and Retreat*; Blue and Gray Press a division of Book Sales, Inc. 1985; p. 41
[xlii] Davis, Burke, *Jeb Stuart – The Last Cavalier*; Wings Books, 1957; p. 191
[xliii] ibid; p. 192
[xliv] B&L; [xliv] Hill, Daniel Harvey, Lieutenant General, C.S.A., *The Battle of South Mountain, Fighting For Time at Turner's and Fox's Gaps*; p. 560
[xlv] Davis; p. 189
[xlvi] *McClellan Papers {C-7:63}*; Library of Congress; United States of America
[xlvii] Sears, Stephen W., *George B. McClellan: The Young Napoleon*; Ticknor & Fields 1988; p. 276; footnote p. 443
[xlviii] Farwell, Byron, *Stonewall - A Biography of General Thomas J. Jackson*; W.W. Norton & Company, 1993, p. 428
[xlix] ibid; p. 428 - 9
[l] Brown, Edmund R.; *The Twenty-seventh Indiana volunteer infantry in the war of the rebellion 1861 to 1865, First division, 12th and 20th corps by a member of Company C.*;1899; all four quotes from p. 226-228
[li] Sears, Stephan W., *Landscape Turned Red*; Popular Library, Warner Books, Inc., 1983 p. 123, hereafter referred to as LTR
[lii] Fishel, Edwin C., *The Secret War for the Union - The Untold Story of Military Intelligence in the Civil War*; Houghton Mifflin Company, 1996, p. 222
[liii] Bowers, John, *Stonewall Jackson - Portrait of a Soldier*; William Morrow & Co.1989; p. 299
[liv] Sears, Stephen W., editor, *The Civil War Papers of George B. McClellan*; Ticknor & Fields; 1989, p. 434
[lv] Colgrove, Silas, Brevet Brigadier-General, U.S.V., *The Finding of Lee's Order*; B&L Vol. II; p. 603 – all three quotations.
[lvi] *B&L Vol. II*; p. 603
[lvii] *LTR*; p. 124
[lviii] ibid; p. 603
[lix] ibid
[lx] Freeman, Douglas Southhall, *Lee's Lieutenants* Vol. II; Charles Scribner 1948, p. 718
[lxi] *Sears*; p. 282
[lxii] Frye, Dennis E., *The General's Tour – Stonewall Attacks – The Siege of Harpers Ferry*; Blue and Gray Magazine; August-September 1987; p. 18
[lxiii] *LTR*; p. 385
[lxiv] *Sears*; p. 280 & 282
[lxv] *Fishel*; p. 239
[lxvi] *Fishel*; p. 240
[lxvii] *Fishel*; p. 238
[lxviii] *B&L Vol. II*; p. 560
[lxix] Huyette, Miles Clayton, *The Maryland Campaign and the Battle of Antietam*; Buffalo, N.Y. 1915, p. 21
[lxx] *B&L Vol. II; p. 564-565*
[lxxi] ibid; p. 565
[lxxii] ibid; p. 563
[lxxiii] ibid; p. 566
[lxxiv] ibid; p. 566-567
[lxxv] ibid; p. 570
[lxxvi] *Sears*; p. 285
[lxxvii] B&L; p.594 - William B. Franklin, Major General United States Volunteers, *Notes on Cramton's Gap and Antietam*
[lxxviii] Howard, H.E., *The Charlottesville*, article entitled *Lee, Lynchburg, and Johnson's Bedford Artillery*; Lynchburg, Virginia, 1990; p.139
[lxxix] *LTR*, p.159
[lxxx] *B&L Vol. II*; p. 580
[lxxxi] ibid; p. 605 - John G. Walker, Major General, C.S.A., *Jackson's Capture of Harpers Ferry*
[lxxxii] Bridges, Hal, *Lee's Maverick General*, McGraw Hill Publishing; 1961; p. 96
[lxxxiii] *LTR*; Appendix I; *The Lost Order*; p.381

Evidential Details

[lxxxiv] *Fishel*, p. 223; "For Lee's comment, see Murfin, *Gleam of Bayonets*, p 337
[lxxxv] *B&L Vol. II*; p. 559
[lxxxvi] Wert, Jeffery D., *General James Longstreet - The Confederacy's Most Controversial General. A Biography*; Simon and Schuster, 1993, p. 93
[lxxxvii] Haskell, John Cleves, *The Haskell Memoirs*; G.P. Putnam's Sons; 1960; p.45
[lxxxviii] *Bridges*; Longstreet's statement p. 149
[lxxxix] *B&L Vol. II*; p.560
[xc] *Longstreet Papers*, Duke University Library; D.H. Hill's letter to James Longstreet, Feb. 11, 1885
[xci] Symonds, Craig L., *Joseph E. Johnston - A Civil War Biography*; W.W. Norton, 1992, p. 142
[xcii] *Daniel Harvey Hill, Jr. Papers*, North Carolina Division of Archives and History, Raleigh, N.C.; Letter from C.D. Fishburne to D.H. Hill, Jr., Chancellorsville, VA. Feb. 8, 1890; p. 1
[xciii] *Bridges*; p. 6
[xciv] *Wilmington Messenger*, September 27, 1889
[xcv] ibid; p. 573
[xcvi] ibid; p. 570
[xcvii] *Lee Papers*, Library of Congress, Lee to D.H. Hill, February 21, 1868.
[xcviii] *B&L Vol. II*; 'The Opposing Forces in the Maryland Campaign'; p. 603
[xcix] *Sears*; p. 325
[c] Sears, Stephen W., *The Civil War Battlefield Guide* "Antietam Chapter"; Houghton Mifflin Company; 1990; p. 86
[ci] Military Commission appointed September 23, 1862; presided over by Major General David Hunter pursuant to War Department General's Office Order 183; *Conclusionary statement* signed by order of the Secretary of War, Assistant Adjutant-General E. D. Townsend, dated Washington D.C. November 8, 1862; Library of Congress
[ci] LS, Lincoln Papers, Library of Congress. OR, Ser. 1, XI, Part 1, pp.73-74

Civil War Bibliography

Battles and Leaders of the Civil War, Vol. II. Castle 1887
--- Hill, Daniel Harvey, Lieutenant General, C.S.A., *The Battle of South Mountain, or Boonsboro*
--- Hill, Daniel Harvey, Lieutenant General, C.S.A., *The Battle of South Mountain, Fighting For Time at Turner's and Fox's Gap*
--- Colgrove, Silas, Brevet Brigadier-General, U.S.V., *The Finding of Lee's Order*
--- William B. Franklin, Major General United States Volunteers, *Notes on Crampton's Gap and Antietam*
--- John G. Walker, Major General, C.S.A., *Jackson's Capture of Harpers Ferry*
--- Editors, The Opposing Forces in the Maryland Campaign
Bowers, John, *Stonewall Jackson - Portrait of a Soldier*; William Morrow & Co. Inc. 1989
Bridges, Hal, *Lee's Maverick General*, McGraw Hill Publishing; 1961
Brown, Edmund R.; *The Twenty-seventh Indiana volunteer infantry in the war of the rebellion, 1861 to 1865, First division, 12th and 20th corps, by a member of Company C.* 1899
Daniel Harvey Hill, Jr. Papers, North Carolina Division of Archives and History, Raleigh, N.C. 1890
Davis, Burke, *Jeb Stuart – The Last Cavalier*; Wings Books, 1957
Farwell, Byron, *Stonewall - A Biography of General Thomas J. Jackson*; W.W. Norton & Company, 1993
Fishel, Edwin C., *The Secret War for the Union - The Untold Story of Military Intelligence in the Civil War*; Houghton Mifflin Company; 1996
Freeman, Douglas Southhall, *Lee's Lieutenants* Vol. II; Charles Scribner & Son's; 1948
Haskell, John Cleves, *The Haskell Memoirs*; G.P. Putnam's Sons; 1960
Hood, J.B., Lt. Gen, CSA, *Advance and Retreat*; Blue and Gray Press, a division of Book Sales, Inc.; 1985
Lee Papers, Library of Congress; February 21, 1868
The Longstreet Papers, Duke University Library

Evidential Details

Library of Congress; United States of America
--- *McClellan Papers {C-7:63}*
--- War Department Office Order 183; Conclusionary statement Assistant Adjutant-General - -
--- E.D. Townsend, Washington D.C. November 8, 186
   Sears, Stephen W., *George B. McClellan: The Young Napoleon*; Ticknor & Fields; 1988
--- *Landscape Turned Red*; Popular Library, Warner Books, Inc.; 1983
--- *The Civil War Papers of George B. McClellan*; Ticknor & Fields; 1989
--- *The Civil War Battlefield Guide* "Antietam Chapter"; Houghton Mifflin Company; 1990
--- Symonds, Craig L., *Joseph E. Johnston - A Civil War Biography;* W.W. Norton; 1992
--- War of the Rebellion: The Official Records of the Union and Confederate Armies, Vol. XIX, Part ii, U.S. Government Printing Office 1880
-- Wert, Jeffery D., *General James Longstreet - The Confederacy's Most Controversial General. A Biography*; Simon and Schuster; 1993

Magazines & Newspapers

--- Frye, Dennis E., *The General's Tour – Stonewall Attacks – The Siege of Harpers Ferry*; <u>Blue and Gray Magazine</u>; August-September 1987
--- Howard, H.E., <u>The Charlottesville</u>, article entitled *Lee, Lynchburg, and Johnson's Bedford Artillery*; Lynchburg, Virginia
--- <u>Wilmington Messenger</u>, September 27, 1889

Custer & Crazy Horse

[ciii] Gilbert, Martin, *Atlas of Russian History*; Oxford University Press, 1993; p. 44
[civ] Crabb, Jr., Cecil V. *American Foreign Policy in the Nuclear Age – Third Edition*, Harper and Row, Publishers, 1972; p. 1
[cv] Crabb; p. 2
[cvi] Custer, George Armstrong, Custer; *My Life on the Plains*, Chapter Two; The LibriVox Free Audio book Collection 2011 hereafter referred to as *Custer*.
[cvii] Crabb; p. 11
[cviii] Richardson, James D., a compilation, *Messages and Papers of the Presidents* – The Peace Policy of President Grant, Extract from his Second Annual Message to Congress December 5, 1870; 7:109-10
[cix] *Custer*, Chapter Two
[cx] *Annual Report of the Board of Indian Commissioners*; United States Printing Office; November 23, 1869; p. 5-11
[cxi] *Custer*, Chapter Two
[cxii] *Custer*, Chapter Two
[cxiii] Utley, Robert M., *Frontier Regulars – The United States Army and the Indian 1866 – 1891*; Macmillan Publishing Co., Inc. 1973; p. 254
[cxiv] Ibid; p. 46
[cxv] Utley; p. 51
[cxvi] *Custer*, Chapter Two
[cxvii] Ibid; p. 52
[cxviii] Hatch, Tom, *Custer and the Battle of the Little Bighorn – An Encyclopedia*; McFarland & Company, Inc., Publishers, 1997; p.168
[cxix] Ambrose, Stephen E., *Crazy Horse and Custer- The Parallel Lives of Two American Warriors*; New American Library – A Meridan Book 1975; p. 417
[cxx] Welch, James with Paul Stekler, *Killing Custer - The Battle of the Little Bighorn and the Fate of the Plains Indians*, W.W. Norton 1994; p.72
[cxxi] Utley; p. 269
[cxxii] Utley, Robert M., *Cavalier in Buckskin*; University of Oklahoma Press 1998; p. 33

Evidential Details

[cxxiii] Ibid; p. 33
[cxxiv] Budiansky, Stephen, *Judging George Custer*; Civil War Times, The Weider History Group, Inc., February, 2011; p. 38
[cxxv] *Custer,* Chapter Three
[cxxvi] Welch/Stekler; p. 173
[cxxvii] Terry, Brigadier General Alfred H., correspondence - Headquarters Department of Dakota, Saint Paul, Minnesota; May 6, 1876 to The Adjutant General, Division of the Missouri, Chicago, Illinois
[cxxviii] Sheridan, Lieutenant General Phillip H., to Brigadier General E. D. Townsend –Washington D.C., May 7, 1976
[cxxix] Sherman, Secretary of War William T. to General A.H. Terry Headquarters of the Army, St Paul, Minnesota, Washington, D.C., May 8, 1976,
[cxxx] Garraty, John A., *The American Nation - A History of the United States Since 1865*; Harper & Row Publishers 1971; p. 31
[cxxxi] The *Marguerite Merington Papers*, Correspondence between Elizabeth Beacon Custer and George Armstrong Custer, June 21, 1876
[cxxxii] Freud ,Sigmund, *The Occult Significance of Dreams* - Collected Papers, Vol. V
[cxxxiii] *Report of the Secretary of War, Executive Documents 1, Part 2*; Forty-fifth Congress, Second session; 1:465 Washing ton D.C.: Government Printing Office 1878; also see Utley, The *Little Bighorn Battlefield – Official National Park Handbook* 132 - Division of Publications, National Park Service; U.S. Department of the Interior, Washington D.C. originally published as *Custer Battlefield*; 1988; p 35-36
[cxxxiv] Terry, General A.H., *Field Diary of General A.H. Terry – Yellowstone Expedition - 1876*; Old Army Press, Second Edition 1970; p. 24
[cxxxv] Ibid; p. 24
[cxxxvi] General Terry's Headquarters field telegrams – Department of Dakota, Camp on Little Big Horn River, Montana, June 27, 1876 to the Adjutant-General of the Military Division of the Missouri, Chicago, Illinois, referred to as TEL
[cxxxvii] Ibid
[cxxxviii] Gray, John S.,*Custer's Last Campaign – Mitch Boyer and the Little Bighorn Reconstructed*; University of Nebraska Press 1991; p. 385
[cxxxix] The Camp Collection; Statement from Two Eagles - 1908
[cxl] Welch/Stekler; p.168
[cxli] *Custer,* Chapter Thirteen
[cxlii] *Graham*; p. 287-95
[cxliii] Taylor, William O., *With Custer on the Little Bighorn - A newly discovered first-person account*; The Penguin Group 1996; Appendix I; p. 177
[cxliv] Graham; p. 73
[cxlv] A.J. Donnelle, *Cyclorama of General Custer's Last Fight Against the Sioux Indians*; Boston Cyclorama Company, 1889; p. 24
[cxlvi] Eastman, C.A., *Rain-In-The-Face: The Story of a Sioux Warrior*; The Teepee Book 1916; p.100
[cxlvii] Fox, Jr., Richard Allan, *Archaeology, History, and Custer's Last Battle;* University of Oklahoma Press, 1993; p. 267
[cxlviii] Welch/Stekler; p.157
[cxlix] *TEL*
[cl] Ibid
[cli] Welch/Stekler; p.164
[clii] Report of the Secretary of War; *The Official Report of General A.H. Terry*; House of Representatives Executive Document 1, Part 2, 44 Congress, 2nd Session, Volume I, Washington, D.C. 1876
[cliii] D. Scott, R. Fox, M. Connor and D. Harmon, *Archaeological Perspectives on the Battle of the Little Bighorn*; University of Oklahoma Press, 1989 p. 281 Human Osteological Remains – Conclusions; p. 86, hereafter referred to as SFCH
[cliv] Scott, Douglas D. and Richard A. Fox Jr., *Archaeological Insights Into the Custer Battle – an Assessment of the 1984 Field Season*; University of Oklahoma Press, 1987; p.123
[clv] Taylor; p.168 from an account written by scout George Herendeen (Bad Heart)

Evidential Details

[clvi] Taylor; p. 76; see also Richard Hardorff, the *Custer Battle Casualties* book p. 21
[clvii] *Archaeological Perspectives*; Interpretation of Indian afterlife belief system as explained by Chief Red Cloud to U.S. Army General Henry B. Carrington.
[clviii] *TEL*
[clix] Headquarters Correspondence - Department of Dakota; Camp on the Yellowstone, near the Big Horn River, Montana, July 2, 1876, to Lieutenant General Phillip Sheridan, Chicago, IL.
[clx] Ambrose; p. 58-9
[clxi] Hardorff, Richard G., *Surrender and Death of Crazy Horse; A Source Book about a Tragic Episode in Lakota History*, A.H.Clark1998; p. 252
[clxii] *SFCH*; p. 281-2

Custer Bibliography

Ambrose, Stephen E., Crazy Horse and Custer- The Parallel Lives of Two American Warriors; New American Library – A Meridan Book 1975
Annual Report of the Board of Indian Commissioners; United States Printing Office; November 23, 1869
Camp Collection; Statement from Two Eagles 1908
Crabb, Jr., Cecil V., American Foreign Policy in the Nuclear Age – 3rd Edition; Foundations of American Foreign Policy; Harper and Row, Publishers 1972
Custer, George Armstrong, Custer; My Life on the Plains; The LibriVox Free Audio Book Collection, 2011
- Donnelle, A.J., Cyclorama of General Custer's Last Fight Against the Sioux Indian; Boston Cyclorama Company 1889
- Eastman, C.A., Rain-In-The-Face: The Story of a Sioux Warrior; The Teepee Book 1916
- Executive Documents 1, Part 2; Report of the Secretary of War, 45th Congress Second session; 1:465 Washington D.C.: Government Printing Office 1878
- Fox, Jr., Richard Allan, Archaeology, History, and Custer's Last Battle, University of Oklahoma Press 1993

Freud, Sigmund, The Occult Significance of Dreams - Collected Papers, v. 5
Garraty, John A., The American Nation - A History of the United States Since 1865; Harper & Row Publishers 1971
Gilbert, Martin, Atlas of Russian History; Oxford University Press 1993
Graham, W.A., The Custer Myth: A Source Book of Custerana; Harrisburg, Pennsylvania 1953
Gray, John S., Custer's Last Campaign – Mitch Boyer and the Little Bighorn Reconstructed; University of Nebraska Press 1991
Hardorff, Richard G., Surrender and Death of Crazy Horse; A Source Book about a Tragic Episode in Lakota History, A.H.Clark 1998
Hatch,Tom, Custer and the Battle of the Little Bighorn – An Encyclopedia; McFarland & Company, Inc., Publishers 1997
Katz, Irving, August Belmont – A Political Biography, Columbia University Press 1968
Nevins, Allan, The War for the Union: War Becomes Revolution. 1862-1863, Konecky & Konecky1960
Official Report of General A.H. Terry; Report of the Secretary of War; House of Representatives Executive Document 1, Part 2, 44 Congress, 2nd Session, Volume I, Washington, D.C. 1876
Richardson, James D., Compilation of Messages and Papers of the Presidents, The Peace Policy of President Grant, Extract from his Second Annual Message to Congress, December 5, 1870
Scott, Fox, Connor and Harmon, Archaeological Perspectives on the Battle of the Little Bighorn; University of Oklahoma Press 1989
Scott, Douglas D. and Richard A. Fox Jr., Archaeological Insights Into the Custer Battle – an Assessment of the 1984 Field Season; University of Oklahoma Press 1987

Evidential Details

Sheridan, Lieutenant General Phillip H., to Brigadier General E. D. Townsend – Washington D.C., May 7, 1876

Sherman, Secretary of War William T., to General A.H. Terry, Headquarters of the Army, St Paul, Minnesota, Washington, D.C., May 8, 1876

Taylor, William O., With Custer on the Little Bighorn - A newly discovered first person account; The Penguin Group 1996

Terry, Brigadier General Alfred Howe
- Correspondence - Headquarters Department of Dakota, Saint Paul, Minnesota; May 6, 1876 to The Adjutant General, Division of the Missouri, Chicago, Illinois
- Telegrams from Terry's field Headquarters – Department of Dakota, Camp on Little Big Horn River, Montana, June 27, 1876 to the Adjutant-General of the Military Division of the Missouri, Chicago, Illinois
- Correspondence - Department of Dakota; Camp on the Yellowstone, Near the Big Horn River, Montana, July 2, 1876, to Lieutenant General Phillip Sheridan, Chicago, Illinois
- Terry's telegrams from his field Headquarters – Department of Dakota, Camp on Little Big Horn River, Montana, June 27, 1876 to the Adjutant-General of the Military Division of the Missouri, Chicago, Illinois
- Field Diary of General A.H. Terry – Yellowstone Expedition – 1876; Old Army Press, Second Edition 1970

Utley, Robert M.,
- Frontier Regulars – The United States Army and the Indian 1866 – 1891; Macmillan Publishing Co., Inc. 1973
- Little Bighorn Battlefield – Official National Park Handbook Division of Publications, National Park Service; U.S. Department of the Interior, Washington D.C. originally published as Custer Battlefield; 1988
- Cavalier in Buckskin; University of Oklahoma Press, 1998

Welch, James with Paul Stekler, Killing Custer - The Battle of the Little Bighorn and the Fate of the Plains Indians; W.W. Norton 1994

Magazines & Papers

Budiansky, Stephen, *Judging George Custer*; Civil War Times, The Weider History Group, Inc., February, 2011

Marguerite Merington Papers; Elizabeth Beacon Custer correspondence to George Armstrong Custer, June 21, 1876

Ricker Tablets; The Yellow Horse interview; Nebraska State Historical Society

Walter Camp Collection; *Custer Battlefield Monument research files*, Crow Agency, Montana; Statement from Thunder Hawk's wife - June 1909

Historians wage a constant battle in trying to pin down reality. How they are being treated by the political, social, or religious pressures in the now of their time and place will usually dictate how they will report reality. Since it is the political, social, and religious environment that pays for their work, endorses their findings, and passes judgment on them, who can blame them for doing otherwise.

Joseph W. McMoneagle - *The Ultimate Time Machine*

www.ingramcontent.com/pod-product-compliance
Lightning Source LLC
Chambersburg PA
CBHW040321300426
44112CB00020B/2830